Happiness is always a by-produc
on securing it... It always come;
of noble things, the things ess
life's journey, with a brave heart, doing the best he can... he often
the faint flutter of invisible wings, he feels a presence, a companion. It
is Happiness. ~*Chicago Herald*, c. 1917

A smile costs nothing but gives much. It enriches those who receive
without making poorer those who give. It takes but a moment, but the
memory of it sometimes lasts forever. None is so rich or mighty that
he cannot get along without it and none is so poor that he cannot be
made rich by it. Yet a smile cannot be bought, begged, borrowed, or
stolen, for it is something that is of no value to anyone until it is given
away. Some people are too tired to give you a smile. Give them one of
yours, as none needs a smile so much as he who has no more to give.
~Author unknown

Our deepest fear is not that we are inadequate. Our deepest fear is that
we are powerful beyond measure. It is our light, not our darkness that
most frightens us. We ask ourselves, Who am I to be brilliant, gorgeous,
talented, fabulous? Actually, who are you not to be? You are a child of
God. Your playing small does not serve the world. There is nothing
enlightened about shrinking so that other people won't feel insecure
around you. We are all meant to shine, as children do. We were born to
make manifest the glory of God that is within us. It is not just in some of
us; it is in everyone. And as we let our own light shine, we unconsciously
give other people permission to do the same. As we are liberated from
our own fear, our presence automatically liberates others. ~Marianne
Williamson, *A Return to Love: Reflections on the Principles of "A Course
in Miracles,"* 1992 (commonly misattributed to Nelson Mandela, 1994
inauguration speech)

Positive thinking does not mean trying to create something that is not
there. Real positive thinking acknowledges that good already exists —
indeed it is *all* that exists. ~Alan Cohen, 1987

My joy may be diminished now, but I am still alive to be more joyful ahead. ~Ankam Nithin Kumar, April 2012 winner of The Quote Garden create your own quote contest on Twitter

You cannot stop trusting people in life but I have learned to be a little bit careful. The way to make people trust-worthy is to trust them. ~Ernest Hemingway, letter to Dorothy Connable, February 17th 1953

"I Have Time for You"

Weekly Affirmations

Lisa Carmichael

Dedicated to the hero deep inside of me who helped me find myself.

Thank you for showing me how safe and secure I could feel.

The Journey Begins…

TABLE OF CONTENTS

INTRODUCTION

What Am I Here to Learn?

Who takes time for themselves? Who has time for themselves? I didn't.

Somehow in my journey of life, I lost myself. Ironically, I didn't realize I went missing—or what I had missed. I knew I had good judgement, but I lacked self-confidence because I did not trust myself.

In reality, my confidence was waiting inside of me, but I was too worried about how I was being perceived. Everything we have experienced has brought us to where we are today. Every experience—good and bad—has made us who we are. Everything was meant to be and has been part of God's plan. My lack of self-confidence came from not trusting myself and from looking outside of me for validation and reassurance.

Now it is entirely possible that you "get it" when it comes to confidence. Maybe you already know how to speak to yourself in a loving manner. Or perhaps you *think* you know how to speak to yourself in a loving manner with positive self-talk. Not everyone understands the power of this concept. Most of us have hang-ups, and we question ourselves about why things are the way they are. Why am I not a billionaire? Why is my skin imperfect? Why am I overweight? Why am I not smart enough? Why can't I stop this behavior?

If these kinds of questions haven't plagued you, or you just don't care, please stop reading right here. This book isn't for you.

For the rest of us, however, please understand the following. *You* are amazing. *You* can find pure happiness and joy because of the dialogue you create in your mind.

Have you ever wondered why you have a certain behavior? It is entirely possible it originated from a recording of negative self-talk… possibly from a recording that you believe no longer affects you. But here's the thing: nothing will ever change until you make time to listen to both your pain and your joy, so you can become the person you have always wanted to be.

If you keep repeating the same thoughts, you can expect that nothing will change for you. You have learned how to walk this journey of life using the repetition of positive and negative thoughts. This is called "mindset." When a person has not acquired the success(s) he desires in any area of life, it is probably time to listen to the heart and examine the mindset.

It is true that we attract everything that we feel inside of us. When we ignore ourselves, we feel unfulfilled. But when I discovered a few vital principles, everything changed. Once I committed to anchoring myself into these seven principles, I was able to find the self-confidence that I never knew existed. It allowed me to step into my true power. This kind of shift is something that I think everyone should experience, so they can begin to realize their own confidence, joy, and success. I want this for *you*! More importantly, *you deserve this*!

In this book, I gift to you my daily affirmations so you can anchor yourself these seven principles in you until they become a part of you. My hope is that knowing these principles and reading these affirmations will help you create your own daily practice of self-talk that you can fall back on. I want you to own these affirmations so they become your own recordings of positive self-talk.

THE SECRET SEVEN

The seven key principles for you to embrace and integrate into your daily life are:

1. Discipline
2. Empowerment
3. Feeling
4. Trust
5. Acceptance
6. Receive
7. Gratitude

Implementing each of these seven principles will bring you closer to understanding your unique purpose. In this book I will be guiding you through these seven principles and helping you unlock each one. But before we can start that rewarding work, we must first take time to understand. This requires an open and vulnerable heart.

Opening up to unconditional love is really what this journey is all about. As wonderful as the outcome is, the journey itself can be a challenge and may feel like an intense struggle. The key to this incredible transformation is the heart. The heart is truly the center of one's confidence. But when there are hurts and unhealed wounds, it's difficult to understand what is impeding our happiness and success.

The truth is that so many people go through their lives with a closed heart that naturally develops from pain we experience. After all, we are simply protecting ourselves from more hurt while unwittingly also blocking out love. *Mostly our wounds and blocks are unconscious. We may think we understand the protection is necessary, but we are still blocked by not realizing the cost of that precious protection.*

What's really hiding in my heart behind all that armored protection? Chances are that life's experiences, both good and bad, are creating those blockages. Ask yourself:

- What is blocking me from fully opening up to me?
- Is old hurt preventing me from feeling truly safe to love and be loved?
- Are fears of abandonment creating secret patterns of self-sabotage?

These seven principles will walk you through embracing the emotions and finding your purpose, confidence, and joy.

On my journey, I have trusted so many people, but I had forgotten to trust myself. I had gone to other people for answers, but I had not looked inside my own heart. The answers came from what I told myself daily. I am responsible for my thoughts, my feelings, and my willingness to open up to myself. The answers I had been searching for had always been inside of me. I was so worried I would make a mistake—or that someone else knew something better. I was filled with guilt, fear, and shame. I was programmed to tell myself with negative thoughts that I wasn't good enough. These are the recordings that I was telling myself. This was all I was hearing inside of my head.

When I was young, I didn't understand the meaning of self-care. My life was about watching others and observing them. It is one thing to be a happy-go-lucky child where everyone loves you. But once we venture into the world around us – for me it was when I started school – reality we notice that others are getting attention instead of ourselves. I questioned if I mattered. I forgot who I was. I wanted to be like everyone else. I felt I wasn't good enough. These other people were happy. They seemed happier than I was. I lost myself and wanted to be like them. I didn't know any better. I really just wanted to fit in.

I kept wondering why couldn't I be as happy as they were. Why wasn't I as pretty? Why didn't everybody love me like they did the others? I lost myself when I started comparing myself to others. Instead of focusing on myself, I was observing others and wishing I could be like one of them. I thought I loved myself, but believed others loved themselves more. *I didn't realize how much I craved being the center of attention.*

It took me a lifetime to realize I needed to find myself. I was the one who needed to honor myself.

Know this: When we focus on developing our best selves, others will be attracted to us naturally. That attention I craved would come organically when I was myself.

I never had the confidence I desired because I wasn't willing to look at myself. I thought my confidence would come from others or even money—things outside myself. And I thought I would be someone important someday, once I had money. I tried writing a diary. Only the negative thoughts came to mind, and that's what showed up on paper. I tried writing daily affirmations. I didn't get it. I was still comparing myself to others. I never believed in myself. I never thought I was worthy.

But I was mistaken, and that is why I am so eager to guide you with these seven principles; to give you a shortcut on the path that took me a long time to learn.

I am grateful for the unconditional love my parents gave me. I was brought into this world because of love. But I was so angry because I didn't understand what love truly meant. The love I needed the most was the love I needed to give myself. We cannot force anyone to love us—but we can love ourselves. We can love ourselves unconditionally. It does not happen overnight. It takes a commitment to yourself to make space for you.

What is my goal? I am here to make a difference.

Steven R. Covey teaches that one habit of highly successful people is to "begin with the end in mind." What is your end? Who do you want to be? When I answered those questions for myself, I decided that I want to be someone who speaks truth. I want to be the person who can genuinely say, "I made a difference today." Even if I'm scared and even if I'm afraid, I show up.

I want to love because I'm a loving person, not because I want to get something. I want to be an example of what love is. Taking action is brave. The most loving thing I can do is be an example.

I want to be bigger than any pain and others will know it through my actions. No one can stop me. No other human being can hold me back. It doesn't matter how much I get hurt. My goal is not to avoid pain; that is "playing small." Playing small doesn't serve me well. My goal is to be a powerful woman for myself and for the people I love, in order to set an example. My self-worth drives me forward.

On my journey, every step has been a piece of the puzzle. I didn't have all the answers, but I had lots of emotions. Surrendering to these emotions pulled my heart in every direction. I craved clarity, but instead I ran away. My emotions were scary, and I was afraid of the future.

Through these seven principles, I have learned that the feelings I experience make me stronger. Handling a crisis from the emotional mind rather than analyzing it intellectually will dramatically shorten its duration.

By trying to block the emotions, the negative thoughts will continue. For example, we all know someone who experienced an emotional crisis years ago and, to this day, do not seem to be able to move beyond that crisis. The trauma seems to persist in their life, and they continue to pay a big price of happiness because they avoid their emotions surrounding the event.

There is an adage that says: fear of life is really the fear of emotions. It is not the facts that we fear, but our feelings about the facts. Once we understand those feelings, our fear of life diminishes. We feel more self-confidence, and we are willing to take greater chances because we have learned that we can handle the emotional consequences, whatever they might be.

Every emotional experience is an opportunity to get bitter or get better. Which do we choose? We have the opportunity to choose whether we want to hang onto or let go of emotional upsets. What pleasure do we hold when we hang on to pain? The part of us that wants to cling to negative emotions is our smallness. Staying small leads us to diminished self-respect. Is that the part we want to re-energize? Is that the way we want to see ourselves? If that's how we want to see ourselves, that's the way others will see us. Have you noticed that when we focus on the negative behaviors of others, we sometimes unconsciously see only those behaviors?

My journey has been a puzzle—a puzzle that took time and commitment to create. Writing in my journal helped me understand my feelings, and this lead to creating positive affirmations. My journal helped me put the pieces together. I was afraid to look at myself. I was looking at everyone else and comparing myself. It was easier looking at others and trying to help them, instead of helping myself. The world can only see us as we see ourselves. It's time to stop resisting the positive emotions. It's time to stop resisting the negative emotions. All the resisting has built barriers that kept my heart blocked from love.

So often I struggle because I think I need approval from others. I ignore my inner child and think I have to suffer because I've been ignored by others. However, I am actually ignoring myself.

Giving myself love, and remembering I am the person who loves me the most, solves the puzzle. I don't need the approval from others to live my life. I live my life because I find my own happiness. I don't need to be afraid. Jesus holds my hand and the Holy Spirit fills my heart with deep love, deep joy, and deep abundance. God has a plan, and I will trust in that plan. I deserve respect, love, and honor. I give myself this. I trust myself. I trust in God's heavenly plan. I am love because I am me. I am magical. I am magnetic. I am soft, sacred feminine energy.

Ask yourself:

- How will it feel when I am in complete harmony with myself?
- What abundance do I need to feel safe in life to open up?
- What does an ideal relationship feel like?
- How would it feel to be free to move forward with joy and harmony in my relationships, including my relationship with myself?

Whatever it feels like, I want to create a future rich in love and joy for myself and for you. We can handle with grace anything that comes our way. Every day it takes courage to be ourselves. We have a choice: to determine who we want to be, or to let the world tell us who we will be.

INSTRUCTIONS – AFFIRMATIONS
AND PERSPECTIVE

"Making time for ME is key..."

What Am I Here to Learn?

As much as I want you to speak positively to yourself every day, there is no right way or wrong way to speak to yourself. There is no judgement. Some days—and even some moments—are better than others. We are all unique. It is so important to accept ourselves.

We get stuck when we start listening to others. When we start listening to other people's opinions, we don't listen to ourselves. If we ask the opinion of others, we will get different answers. My point is that it is time to build confidence in ourselves. If we don't take the time to support the muscles used to build ourselves up, we will stay small.

Every day is a new day. The language we speak to ourselves creates who we are. We are what we believe. If we shut ourselves off from our emotions, we miss out on life. Is this logical? Are we listening to our brains or to our hearts? Our brains want everything organized and logical. Life is about being both logical and emotional. Life is about living. Life is not about making others proud of us. Life is about being proud of ourselves.

Affirmations are a different way of thinking. When we stop eating healthy, stop exercising, or stop telling ourselves positive affirmations, our brain goes back to our old habits. Why would we want to shut ourselves off from living? We have to pick our battles. We have to decide what is most important; and then just live.

If we believe in the good things in life and have faith, abundance will automatically be attracted to us. If we live life how we think others want us to live, we will never find our confidence. Our confidence comes from trusting that God has a plan, and knowing everything will be okay. When we get stuck, Jesus holds our hand without us even knowing it.

What's the point of journaling? Why not face those fears and acknowledge them? When we write down what's happening, it gives us an understanding. This all takes time. What are you willing to make time for? What is your priority? If we want change and if we want confidence (that is why you're reading this, right), it doesn't happen overnight. It's a process.

We take one step at a time. We start each day feeding our soul with positive affirmations. We make time for ourselves. We make time to honor the hero inside of ourselves to find our courage.

My hero is deep inside of myself. Every day my hero needs to be reminded what to believe. My hero shows me how safe and secure I can feel. When we can love ourselves, we become that hero. A superhero. The time we give to our hero is priceless.

I followed a simple and easy-to-use system. I discovered these seven principles of *discipline, empowerment, feeling, trust, acceptance, receive,* and *gratitude.* Each day I tried to understand how I could use one of these principles to build my confidence. The first step was making the time to follow this thought process. Every morning I give myself the gift of time.

Not that I truly understood where my time belonged, I simply created a system of focusing on one principle every morning. Each morning, like being faithful to an exercise program, I made time to remind myself where my confidence comes from. If you aren't willing to take the time to communicate with yourself what you want in life, nothing will change.

This is for you to find yourself the way I have. These daily affirmations will allow you to face the negative—and then manifest the positive that you deserve. You deserve everything you desire! These are seeds to be planted. This can be your garden.

GETTING STARTED

What Am I Here to Learn?

Writing affirmations will move you in the right direction of changing what's been blocking you. These affirmations will prompt you to look deep inside yourself for inspiration. It's frustrating, I agree. These affirmations can be journal prompts to inspire you to dig deeper so you can build a mind-set muscle. I promise you that it won't happen overnight. It will take a commitment to the process. With practice and repetition, you will learn how to heal, and also how you can attract all the good things you desire.

However, the first step is to take action. The most important part is getting started. Find a time to start, preferably your first thoughts of the day when your mind is clear—before you look at social media or any messages. The first step is the simple action of making time. This is your time to focus on you. It is so important to focus on your routine as you get started. Attach to the process and detach from the outcome. Your commitment is seven days a week and 52 weeks a year.

This is discipline, which is an emotion that might scare you. Discipline is one of the key principles. Consider this:

- Every morning as soon as you wake, pull out your affirmations because then your mind is clear.
- Commit to reading the affirmations every single morning.
- Read the affirmations quietly or out loud.
- Soon you will create your own affirmations.
- Follow my lead and also create your own journal.
- Find your inspiration.

Next, let the words flow and never hold back. Let your heart flow through your pen or keyboard. This is where you share your true feelings—and nothing less. Think of your journal as a safe place to express yourself. It's your place to keep your innermost thoughts. It's a place where you won't have to worry about being judged. These are your thoughts and, soon to be, your inspiration.

Traditionally, a journal is a small notebook. I found a cheap spiral composition notebook that works for me. There are a variety of digital options available and any sort of program will work. Dating your entries allows you to go back and review your thoughts.

Keeping a diary or a journal is good exercise. However, there will likely come a day when you're not feeling inspired. Or worse, a day when you realize only the negative thoughts flow freely out of your mind. Writing won't always come easy. Remember, you're committed to this journey because you want to find what is holding you back. You desperately want to find your confidence. That is your end result, right?

The combination of your commitment of processing daily affirmations by reading or writing them in your journal is key. Together with all of these seven principles, you will come closer to finding yourself and realizing that there is hero inside of you waiting to be heard. This is a commitment to you. There are seven principles for you to follow. As you go throughout the week, it is your choice of how you want to repeat these principles. You have the freedom to roll the weeks together—or focus on a different principle each day. It's okay to repeat a principle or skip a principle, but it's not okay to skip a day. You're creating a habit that is building character. The other two days are your free days to repeat and reflect.

PRINCIPLE #1: DISCIPLINE

What Am I Here to Learn?

Discipline will come when there are no expectations. Through discipline, we are teaching ourselves better boundaries. Some may feel that discipline is a privilege. I grew up feeling that discipline meant judgment. There are moments when I know I "should" take action—but I would prefer not to. I would rather avoid my responsibilities and hope for the best. Taking action is just energy. This energy is waiting to serve us. When we commit to taking action, we feel good about the outcome. When we are willing to follow-through on our responsibilities and take action, this is discipline. Some might call it "masculine energy."

Solving problems, getting things done, thinking, analyzing, over-analyzing, and looking for solutions are all masculine energy, and each one requires discipline.

When we are afraid to take action, we are most fearful of the consequences. Surrendering to our discipline allows us to take action, which brings abundance. Why are we afraid of this abundance? If we don't understand what could be next, we can't predict. Predicting the future is not where we have control. We have control only over our actions. Logic allows us to create conclusions for our assumptions. Logic helps us create patterns of both good and bad reasoning—so know which patterns to follow and which to avoid.

Truth comes from logical understanding. Logic is a simple system with a set of principles. Logic helps us understand. One might say truth comes from logically designed principles. It's our reasoning. Logic is also a discipline. Logic tells us how to reason. Finding confidence will come when you follow these principles for affirmations.

Discipline requires waiting and not getting frustrated. Empowerment comes from trusting that everything will be okay, and reminding ourselves of this truth. Every emotion is worth acknowledging. Acknowledging that every emotion we feel is valid brings us closer to our truth. Our truth helps us find our confidence. Our confidence does not come from the outside. It comes from trusting and having discipline. Getting emotional and frustrated doesn't serve us. However, these are not wasted energies. Fulfillment comes from feeling every emotion—even frustration.

These affirmations are given to help you create a habit of becoming positive by working through your emotions. We all make mistakes; it's our choice whether to learn from them. No matter who we are, life is going to put us through the changes we need to go through. The question is: are we willing to use these affirmations for our transformation?

What are these principles of reasoning that are part of our logic? There are many such principles. Actually, it's your choice. I have chosen the principles of DISCIPLINE, EMPOWERMENT, FEELING, TRUST, ACCEPTANCE, RECEIVE, and GRATITUDE. These are all emotions that help us build our confidence. This is a journey. I will be the first to say it is not easy to understand, and it's definitely okay that you don't understand and are confused. Because this is a journey, the principle you choose will guide you. There is beauty in allowing yourself to be vulnerable and in finding compassion when you don't understand.

Creating this manuscript has brought so much discipline into my life—more than I ever anticipated or imagined. Writing this book has been a huge frustration. I have been frustrated with completing this "work of art." I've spent my entire life waiting for answers from someone else—literally. (Decision making is not my strength.) The one emotion I wasn't facing is anger.

As a child, anger was an emotion that was actually allowed—which is not typical. We were allowed to feel our emotions. As a child, I internalized everything until I blew up like a hot tea kettle. I knew I would complete this book. That's my personality. If I start something, I finish it. This time I haven't been able to walk away from the end of my story. Why was my heart so heavy? When I finally faced my anger yesterday and blew up, I realized I never learned boundaries, or at least boundaries when it comes to frustration. I was talking myself out of showing my anger.

My heart was hurting. As I have written this book, I have hoped that readers would find worth in its content so they improve their own lives by practicing these principles. But I wasn't willing to face my fear that my audience would not benefit from my work. This time, walking away from the pain without facing my fear and my anger was not healthy. This was not self-pity. This was my reality. Was I special? We are all special. We get to choose how we feel.

Have you ever spent an entire day waiting for an answer? I did this recently, and I internalized the problem. I blew up. I gave myself a headache because I was so angry. I may have destroyed some brain cells. I internalized the problem and started focusing on how angry I was getting. I made myself feel angry. I was frustrated. I had only tears and anger to comfort me.

The next day, I started fresh. I forgive myself. The pain I experienced the day before was horrible. Procrastination had not served me. It was time to let go of the anger and be okay with where things would land. I learned a new boundary. Talking myself out my anger did not serve me.

I am not a therapist. I am not a life coach. I'm simply a mom who has learned some tough lessons along the way and hopes to make difference in your life. Have I chosen a difficult path? Perhaps. Seems like I often do.

I've talked myself out of anger, or maybe after getting angry I felt guilt. Writing this book has been a huge frustration. I write from my heart, but maybe you need some real-life proof. Here is a little more insight into me and my journey.

Walking away from pain without facing it is not healthy. I find I can be easily offended, especially if I choose to ignore myself. Why does my heart get so heavy? Sadly, I internalize everything. I try to make everyone happy and it simply is not possible. I never learned the boundaries of letting go. I only knew self-pity. One time, I spent the entire day waiting for answers from someone else. But I was so stressed out about the wait that I wanted to run away. I reasoned that if I walked away, I was selfish. I tend to internalize every problem and delay addressing my emotions until all I have left is tears and anger. It has always been the worst feeling in the world. Procrastination never serves me. It frustrates me to no end. I have learned that I deserve better. I deserve abundance.

Back to that first step. Ask yourself:

- How serious are you about changing?

- How open are you to finding your confidence and your self-esteem?
- How open are you to building your confidence?
- What steps are you taking to build your confidence?

I chose to show up for myself every single morning, repeating my affirmations. Imagine the feeling if you created a boundary in your life by utilizing your own affirmations or by following mine. Because of my deep commitment to repeating my daily affirmations, I am bringing more love to my life and to the thing empowering me. You can too!

Commit to your journey of self-affirmations. Your time is valuable. If your time is limited one day or you're feeling stuck during the day, pick through a few of these to remind yourself what is imaginable.

1. I've discovered this journey.
2. I'm emotionally stronger.
3. I know I need to be a better communicator.
4. I have realized that vulnerability is my strength.
5. Only I can make myself happy.
6. I use my masculine energy in a new way.
7. I feel more worthy.
8. I love my "inner child" more.
9. I am committed to journaling.
10. I am committed to meditating.
11. I have a deeper love for myself.
12. I have a deeper love for others.
13. I trust my intuition more.
14. I've built stronger friendships with others.
15. I have more compassion.
16. I am celebrating me.
17. I trust myself more.
18. I've reached out to others.
19. I've created boundaries around social media.
20. I've created healthy boundaries around sleep.
21. I'm the only person who can love me.
22. I'm the one who has to fill this void.

23. I've discovered my magnetic energy.

24. I've discovered I deserve abundance.

25. I have more opportunity for growth.

26. I'm learning empowerment.

27. I'm getting closer to working with the right people.

28. I've had amazing growth.

29. This is setting me up to find better friends.

30. This is making me a better friend.

31. My mind has been opened to my surroundings.

32. I'm trying to funnel this energy into other people.

33. It's helped me realize my value.

34. I'm more independent.

35. I'm grounding myself more.

36. I love myself more.

37. I'm connecting with myself more.

38. I am practicing new skills.

39. I am eating healthier.

40. I attract more healthy relationships.

41. My tolerance has changed.

42. I have a better spiritual relationship with myself.

43. I trust God differently and better.

44. My energy has changed.

45. I'm comfortable with my feelings.

46. I've felt an energy I never knew existed.

47. I have more courage.

48. I can trust God's plan.

49. I know how to pull inward.

50. I can be me.

51. Good energy is my guide.

52. I am doing things for me.

PRINCIPLE #2: EMPOWERMENT

What Am I Here to Learn?

When I was 21, I struggled with my identity once again. I had poor self-esteem and a poor body image. I gained the "freshman 15" (some weight), and I was self-conscious. I felt alone and was definitely struggling with my identity. I wasn't attractive. It didn't help having the memories of being teased or bullied when I was a youth. I thought I was invincible. I began the binge-and-purge self-help concept. I loved food, but it was a terrible relationship. I was so proud of myself that I could eat anything… and throw up anything. There was no reason for this behavior, or at least I did not think so. It made me feel good to show others I could eat whatever I wanted. I had no self-control. I had no boundaries. A behavior like this had not been heard of, and thus it was ignored. Years ago, the generation before me assumed things like this would go away on their own. Fortunately, I found a book about bulimia at a bookstore. I discovered I had an eating disorder. I was too embarrassed at what I was doing to my body. I remember the book explaining all the side effects what could result from bulimia, like facial hair and dark-end teeth. Later on I discovered the proper way to lose weight and keep it off. Trust me, it wasn't cheap, and it wasn't easy. I knew it was important to be healthy and look healthy so I made the commitment of journaling my meals and working with trained professionals. So ironically, that was one of my first exposures to keeping a journal. The accountability from a trained professional and my out-of-pocket expense helped me with that discipline.

The Principle of Empowerment

This concept of journaling begins with the principle of empowerment. As we go through our moments in life, we forget to exist. We focus on solving our problems rather than embracing all the feelings and sensations around us. In every moment there is an experience. When we eat, we experience taste and flavor. However, the practice of eating can be associated with the pleasures of taste, smell, and touch, as well as other behaviors and emotions. When we view food and eating as *only a survival mechanism*, we miss the experience. Without processing our experiences, we miss out on the emotions that life is offering us. Our mind wants only survival, and chooses to ignore the intensity. What is this intensity? The intensity of flavor determines the degree of hunger and desire. The blood flow in certain areas of the brain are increased. When the flow to the brain changes, we can begin to notice the change we feel in our body.

Experiencing the moment relates to the intensity of the feelings you are willing to acknowledge. Have you ever stopped to think about what you're experiencing in the moment right now? Maybe you're confused, maybe you're frustrated, maybe you're sad? Whatever you are experiencing, the concept of journaling and creating positive affirmations will teach you how to love yourself in a positive way. Shutting ourselves off from our emotions does not serve us.

I've discovered that there are studies that prove the brain has the ability to distinguish different components of our feelings. Our brain's activity around temperature and pain transfers throughout our body. It's safe to assume that more research is being done on the relationship between brain activity and the different connections based on the physiological feelings. Obviously, this is my own theory because these same experiences can be felt in all of our senses. When we choose to slow down and listen to the tempo of the sounds around us, I've learned that we create a magnetic energy because the blood flows differently throughout our body. We allow ourselves to feel the intensity of these sensations, or when we are in a conversation, we can acknowledge the vibrations we are receiving through the communication. When we shut off our brain from thinking and solving, it helps us to embrace the moment in front of us.

I wish I could teach you how important it is to stay in the moment. It's not a discipline that happens overnight. It takes years of practice. By journaling and writing my own affirmations, I was able to practice this over and over again. I built my confidence through repetition. I repeated these affirmations to remind myself the importance of staying in the moment so I could experience life's sensations.

As an example, I never understood why I was afraid to open up to other people. I took pride in staying private. My silence would instead speak volumes. By staying private I was pretending to be someone I was not. However, this made others perceive me as negative. The spiral effect was that I didn't trust others. I was too afraid to open my heart. Neither transparency nor vulnerability were in my vocabulary. Through my daily affirmations and the habit I created, I started showing up for myself every day. I proved to myself that I was trustworthy. This allowed me to view others as trustworthy.

PRINCIPLE #3: FEELING

What Am I Here to Learn?

Most people will write in a diary in order to transfer their feelings onto paper. Others will completely avoid journaling because *they don't want to transfer their feelings onto paper.* Could it be a risk to journal those thoughts—or is that just a misconception? For most, journaling is too emotional to even begin. When we are afraid of something, our hearts begin to race, our mouths become dry, our skin turns pale, or our muscles contract. These emotional reactions occur automatically and unconsciously. Feelings occur after we become aware, and that's when we experience the feeling of fear, shame, guilt, or even depression. In neuroscience, emotions are the reactions the body has to certain situations. Neuroscience will claim that emotions are the reactions the body has to certain situations.

My challenge to you is to journal the emotions of wanting to journal. Solutions don't come when we're stuck in our heads. Journaling embraces those feelings that will help you connect to the deeper feelings. The feelings we experience make us stronger. Our awareness is anchored to our feelings. When we experience these feelings, we create strength. These affirmations will help you get started. If you have no idea what you're feeling, that's okay. It will happen. But your first step is action. Read the affirmations over and over until you start understanding that your own feelings are legitimate. *As you honor your feelings, you will honor your heart. By honoring your heart, you will find your purpose. And understanding your purpose is where you will find yourself and your confidence.*

I encourage you to make time for yourself every morning—five minutes, ten minutes, thirty minutes or an hour—to acknowledge your feelings. If you don't have any idea what I'm talking about, then read my daily affirmations until you're ready to create your own.

PRINCIPLE #4: TRUST

What Am I Here to Learn?

Healthy relationships begin with trust. The point of building trust is for others to believe what you say. Keep in mind, however, that *building trust requires not only keeping the promises you make, but also not making promises you're unable to keep.* Keeping your word shows others what you expect from them, and in turn, they'll be more likely to treat you with respect, developing further trust in the process. When others follow through on their commitments to us, it makes us trust them. That's where trust develops.

Now we need to build trust in ourselves. When we show up for ourselves and keep commitments to ourselves, that's how we create trust in ourselves. I am building trust in myself by keeping my own commitments to myself and making them a top priority, like journaling, meditation, paying bills, and showing up on time. Building trust begins on the inside. I've learned as I become more trusting in myself, I become more trusting in my relationships.

As I journal and create positive affirmations, I am building trust in myself first. My commitment to my journal and creating positive affirmations builds trust. If I show up for myself, I am building trust. By trusting myself and trusting in God's plan, I am becoming a deeper soul. Trusting that everything will be okay is trusting my intuition. Trusting my intuition builds my confidence. *Every day I remind myself I am trustworthy.* When I choose not to show up for myself, I begin to lose trust in myself again. Today, I choose to show up for myself every single morning to create a stronger mindset, which will build my confidence. I choose to show up for me because I am trustworthy. This principle is another reminder of my commitment to becoming better.

PRINCIPLE #5: ACCEPTANCE

What Am I Here to Learn?

In every single moment we are in "a state of allowing." Allowing is a crucial principle in receiving everything we desire in life. The opposite of allowing is trying to force things to happen. When we allow things to happen organically, things will fall together naturally. All the things we want to experience in our lives are waiting for us; we need to learn how to allow them in. When we are aligned and empowered in our core values, we are in a state of acceptance. *Everything we desire will make its way into our life, when we trust and allow.* When we have faith that everything is working out, abundance is being attracted toward you. The path to acceptance is trusting that everything is working out. Knowing that everything is okay, brings us into the state of acceptance.

Positive affirmations will build the power inside of us to accept everything we desire. All of our desires are waiting to be delivered to us. It's our responsibility to be open to receiving those desires. When we surrender to what we are given, everything happens for our own well-being. When we understand that our energy is a full-body experience, we naturally attract the abundance we want to allow. This creates the energy of fullness rather than the negative energy of being in a place of scarcity.

Repeating our daily affirmations allows us to make peace with ourselves. We are in a state of allowing when we show up for ourselves for positive self-talk. When we choose to believe that these affirmations will work positively in our lives, we are creating a magnetic energy to attract everything we desire. You are attracting fullness rather than coming from a place of weakness. It's powerful to understand that we are given everything we need. In my reading, I discovered there actually is a science behind the idea that *we are what we think.*

By practicing the daily positive affirmations over and over again, we become a magnet for everything we desire without forcing anything or anyone. When we are in a state of acceptance, we are the creators of everything we desire. By being open to acceptance, we are open to allowing everything we desire. Start repeating the affirmations until you have your own positive recordings so you can allow everything you desire.

PRINCIPLE #6: RECEIVE

Receiving is a principle of being open to what is offered without any conditions. Receiving is the most natural way to have what you desire. As we breath, we are receiving life. Notice how it feels to take a breath. Letting yourself receive the breath is not a forced action. It happens naturally. We are receiving our energy with no expected outcome because we know everything will be okay. We are worthy of receiving breath with no worries. We are meant to thrive with every single breath.

It is the same with receiving things into your life. Life is always offering us opportunities to receive what we desire. Receiving starts with self-care. When we take care of ourselves, we are building confidence. The ability to receive is powerful. Knowing I am worthy, makes me a good receiver. Every breath we receive, we are worthy of receiving that breath. Just as it is natural to breathe, it is natural to receive abundance. Everything we desire is being given to us, it's our responsibility to be open to receiving those opportunities. When we can notice the daily challenges, we are receiving wisdom, and are being given opportunities for growth. Understanding the challenges are lessons which are meant to bring us closer to finding our confidence. We all have the ability to receive.

It's possible we may not know how to be a good receiver. Because you simply don't know how to be a good receiver doesn't mean you can't receive. Repetition of these affirmations will change the childhood recordings you learned—those about feeling you were unworthy, not good enough, and unlovable. These negative recordings keep you from receiving. You are worthy. It is your truth. You are everything you believe. The repetition of these positive affirmations will remind you of this. Stop listening to your negative thoughts by creating your own new daily affirmations.

Every day look for ways to love yourself. This brings you closer to finding yourself. The more love you feel for yourself, the easier it is to receive. That loving energy will naturally attract to you more and more of what you desire—and then you can receive it. You will find your purpose and your confidence when you fall in love with yourself. Nurturing your heart by practicing these daily affirmations brings you closer to naturally receiving everything you desire. Be committed to having everything you desire—and life will offer more than you can ever imagine. Your openness to receiving makes you a better receiver. Your openness to understanding and practicing it daily will open your heart to this principle.

PRINCIPLE #7: GRATITUDE

You can't turn off gratitude—and who would want to?

My gratitude for this journey has been the most uplifting piece. Every moment I have struggled, I have looked for gratitude. Every bit of happiness in finding gratitude makes everything more vibrant. Gratitude has not been its own affirmation *because I had to find a way to bring it into my life.*

Maybe writing a journal isn't working for you.

Maybe repeating these daily affirmations isn't for you.

We learn many lessons in our lives. I have been in sales for twenty years. Sales is not the field that I imagined for myself. I became a stay-at-home mom after my third child was born. That's when I became an entrepreneur. Growing up I worked hard, and had three jobs while I was in high school. Staying home and being a mother meant I had to recreate myself. I was still looking for happiness on the outside. I wasn't looking for gratefulness, I was too busy. Life wasn't fulfilling yet.

I started working in the retail industry when I failed at being an entrepreneur—more than once. Here is the life lesson I learned though. I was miserable. Working for someone else again was humiliating until I looked for the joy. When I found gratitude, things slowly changed. When I found the joy in helping others and making their lives better, that's how I made peace.

My life lesson taught me that successful sales business people make two sales a day. I was not that driven. Finding myself on the inside wasn't easy because my goal was that now I had to make the lives of two other people better.

You may not be in sales, but my point is for you to find two things to be grateful for every day. Ask yourself, whose life have you made better today? Or whose life can you make better? You might be making your life better by making someone else's life better—there's your two. Instead of choosing negativity or maybe anger, look for the gratefulness around you.

A picture is worth a thousand words. Every day I have taken a photo. I looked for beauty and I looked for love. The beauty came alive because that's what I was feeling. The pictures I took were selected because I was grateful—and I was looking for beauty. I wasn't trying to impress anyone. I was just being me. I wanted to make my hero smile. I found my hero by looking deep into my soul. *God creates so much beauty…but we forget to notice that beauty.*

I found peace with myself and used my eyes to see there is so much to be grateful for. We are trying so hard to impress everyone else, but that's not where our confidence comes from. What if we started a gratefulness movement? Happiness is everywhere you choose to find it. *You can find happiness if you look for it.*

Finally, what if you chose to make only one person smile every day? Gratitude comes when you choose to make someone happy. What if you choose to make yourself happy?

Gratitude raises the vibration of your energy. Choose to live at that higher vibration.

If you live with gratefulness, the abundance keeps flowing into your heart. Each day I ask you to commit to the discipline of writing your affirmations—and find a simple and easy way to be grateful. If you open up your heart, you will find gratitude. The hero inside of you will give you happiness, allowing you to find your self-confidence.

Yes, it's entirely possible that you're stuck or simply don't understand how to be grateful. I give you 52 weeks of ideas of how you can be grateful through affirmations. This is your challenge. Don't overthink. Don't over analyze! Whatever emotion that you are feeling gives you an opportunity to be grateful. Open the door, let it flow inside of your heart. Gratitude will fill you up naturally.

I am not giving you 52 weeks of "gratitude"-themed affirmations. I have started you off with these shorter thought-provoking affirmations below. Good wishes on a joyful job of creating one for each week of the year.

Here are some ideas to kick off your creative juices.

I am grateful for both these big thoughts and little thoughts ….

- My heart has opened.
- I'm not as confused.

- I enjoy my time alone.
- I am learning to trust.
- I know it's okay to admit that sometimes I am afraid.
- Moderation is my choice.
- I don't have to fear losing friendships.
- I am still learning.
- I'm okay.
- I'm not taking this personally.
- I know everything is working out how it is meant to be.
- I need to trust myself more.
- I've discovered my inner goddess.
- I've discovered the Holy Spirit breathes energy through me.
- My heart is my purpose.
- I surrender to my purpose.
- I love myself like no one else can.
- I am learning to be a good receiver.
- I allow only good energy in my life.
- My worth and value is my energy.
- There are others who will appreciate me more now.
- I am the holder of a beautiful and valuable energy.
- I am worthy of receiving good energy.
- God's plan is better than any plan I can create.
- My job as a woman is to be present.
- I am learning to be a better receiver.
- I am getting comfortable with myself.
- I believe in my core value.
- My loving heart makes me a beautiful person.
- My worth comes from within.
- My value has been elevated to a new level.
- I am worthy of anything because I am me.
- The universe is trying to give to me.
- I am manifesting everything I desire.
- I receive my inspiration from the Holy Spirit.
- I am the source of what I create.
- I choose what I radiate.
- My journey is teaching me to be a better friend.

- My strength is waiting for the universe's answer or solution.
- No one else can make me happy; I make me happy.
- I have boundaries.

Be grateful for how you feel and who you are. There are so many simple tricks to remind us who we are and how we can be grateful. Use these "power words" below with no expectations.

- Authority
- Abundance
- Authentic
- Alive
- Beautiful
- Bountiful
- Confident
- Carefree
- Caring
- Calmness
- Compassion
- Delightful
- Devine
- Empathetic
- Energetic
- Engaging
- Encouraging
- Elegant
- Ethical
- Fun
- Friendly
- Feminine
- Generous
- Gracious
- Gleeful
- Glowing
- Grace
- Gentle

- Grateful
- Grounded
- Happy
- Healthy
- Heartfelt
- Honest
- Honor
- Higher Power
- Integrity
- Interesting
- Influencer
- Inspirational
- Joyful
- Joyous
- Kind
- Knowledgeable
- Knowing
- Loved
- Loving
- Leader
- Magnetic
- Merry
- Magical
- Nice
- Optimistic
- Owner
- Powerful
- Posture

- Pristine
- Pretty
- Peppy
- Poise
- Power
- Queen-like
- Regal
- Resilient
- Radiant
- Skillful
- Sweet
- Smart
- Soft
- Sacred
- Sophisticated
- Sweetness
- Transparent
- Teacher
- Teachable
- Terrific
- Timely
- Understanding
- Valuable
- Vulnerable
- Worthy
- Youthful
- Young
- Zany

MAKING TIME FOR THE HERO INSIDE YOU

What Am I Here to Learn?

If you are like me, making time is a personal choice. We all have moments of time. Time is a priority we ignore. By not prioritizing time for ourselves, we sacrifice our self-worth. Being aware of time takes a commitment. Self-affirmations aren't a trade-off for time. When we are intentional with our time, and commit to bringing more joy and abundance into our lives, scheduling time comes easily. If it's worth it to find yourself and find your self-confidence, then it's worth making time every day to change your thoughts by using positive affirmations. If it's a priority, you will make time. If it's not, feel confident that you are making choices that already match your values. My time was based on fear and frustration. I didn't believe I had the time to focus on me.

I never knew how much damage I was causing myself by living in fear. I didn't understand I was the only one holding me back. I lived in fear because I was telling myself all the wrong things. I didn't understand. I would eventually learn that everything in life has something to teach you—and that it is all for your growth. But I was not ready to see that yet. *I started journaling.* Day after day I opened up to my feelings and I forced the words onto paper. I didn't know how to be me. I didn't know how to show up for me. I only knew things like shame, guilt, anxiety, and fear. I changed my mind-set by speaking differently to myself. I acknowledged my heart and I acknowledged my soul. I wrote those feelings on paper.

I finally had compassion for myself. *The most powerful energy is the energy of compassion.* Compassion is love, gentleness, wisdom, softness, patience, acceptance, and forgiveness. Compassion is healing. You believe what you tell yourself. Feminine energy is receptive energy.

Change and transformation can happen in an instant, and it is also ongoing. Creating change in life needs to be honored. Letting go of any timeline—but committing every single moment to stepping into power, stepping into trust, stepping into receptivity, stepping into surrender, stepping into love, and stepping into openness—is a process. Choosing these elevated frequencies over and over again is a learned behavior. It's choosing sacred energy instead of repeatedly choosing the same thing that has kept you down far too long. This means when you mess up, you meet that mess with compassion and love and sacred energy. Therefore, that mess up becomes sacred energy. When you meet the mistake with compassion, the energy heals it and releases the pain.

The more I master my thoughts, I am honoring my heart, and I am honoring my subconscious. Then all the things on the outside are a reflection of how I feel on the inside. The level of positive thoughts that I'm attracted to are my sacred truth, and that's the level that things are attracted to me.

If we continue to tell ourselves negative stories, we will continue to live in fear and desperation. It's time to live our fullest life and embrace all of our emotions. When we embrace the negative emotions, we become stronger and we learn confidence. Love is not something others can give you. It's an energy. You can feel love at any given point by shifting your energy. Forgiving and loving ourselves is essential to being able to accept love. *If we don't feel loveable, we subconsciously sabotage any love others try to give us.*

Instead of escaping these feelings by watching a movie or distracting ourselves with someone else's projection, I found the courage to listen to myself. What messages are you programming yourself with when you turn on the television and watch a movie? What messages are we receiving when we watch episode after episode or movie after movie? We hear recordings of a reality that isn't ours. We deny our own feelings when we watch the actions of others. We miss out on both the pain and the joy that life wants to give us.

Instead of surrounding myself with outside distractions, I journaled my thoughts. I asked, "What does the universe want to give to me? What does the universe want to provide for me? What am I here to learn? How can I change my mindset?"

Instead, it became easier when I chose to commit to myself. Every person has their own challenges. I only have control over my own actions.

I own my power. These are the things that keep me in line with my commitment to me:

1. Gratitude brings us into our sacred energy. What and who are you grateful for? You begin to crave gratitude because it feels good.
2. Affirmations are words. Every word is a code and a frequency. Every time you're writing a word on paper, you're activating its frequency in your body. If you're feeling doubt, write down what you want to happen. This is what's creating energy.
3. When something is not working in your life, write out all your favorite things. You're choosing exactly what you want and you're alchemizing it in your body. Start noticing.
4. Visualize your future. The subconscious mind, which is the feminine energy, creates everything. Whatever is planted from the outside, you're planting in the subconscious mind. Your outer world is a reflection of your inner world.
5. Understanding my energy. I am soft, sacred feminine energy. My self-confidence comes from my feminine power. My feminine energy is magnetic. Everything I desire is being attracted to me. My empowered life does not come from the external world. My hero is deep inside of myself. Every day my hero needs to be reminded what to believe. My hero shows me how safe and secure I can feel. When we can love ourselves, we become a hero—a superhero. The time that we give to our hero is priceless.

QUESTIONS

What Am I Here to Learn?

Sometimes we lose our purpose in life. Some days we just lose track of time. The morning will fly by, and we can barely account for what we did with our time.

Getting stuck is no fun. When things don't make sense, we can over-analyze and overthink. However, staying stuck is not the solution. I was fortunate enough to be a parent. Life couldn't have ever prepared me for all of the accountability that role requires and involves. I discovered the easiest way to learn the truth is by seeking to understand.

The best advice I can give you—or anyone—is to teach yourself to ask, "*What am I here to learn?*" Life is a lesson waiting for us to learn what is next. When we can take a step back, that's a simple way to stop overthinking. If we trust everything is always working out for us, then when we ask ourselves what are we here to learn, the answers show up on their own.

Overthinking would actually be related to worry, in my opinion. If I can't relax or if I can't shut off my brain, I know I am overthinking again—which turns into this vicious downward spiral. It's hard to recognize it when you're in the middle of it. My brain will try to convince me that worry is somehow helpful. Worry about the past or the future, is not something I have control over.

Building my confidence comes from facing the facts. Solutions come when we let go of any attachment. Our worry creates a control mechanism. Overthinking involves dwelling on the problem. When we dwell on the problem, we feel bad that we don't have control, and this creates negativity.

Overthinking is different than self-reflection. Healthy self-reflection is about learning something about yourself in order to gain a new perspective about a situation. It's purposeful. Self-reflection offers new insight.

Overthinking won't prevent bad things from happening. We must recognize that overthinking does more harm than good. For me personally, overthinking does nothing to prevent or solve my problems.

For example, as I finish this manuscript, I need to find a proofreader. I am so worried about the outcome and choosing the right candidate, I ignore my feelings and worry that I may make a poor choice. Obviously, I have moved forward and chosen someone. I took action which helped me publish this book. The worry I had about this decision cost me more time, which caused me more frustration because I didn't have time to work on the new things in life that needed my attention.

If you struggle with your affirmations, I encourage you to ask yourself the questions below as you self-reflect. Remember, you are asking these questions to open yourself up to your willingness about what you are here to learn.

Sometimes we have to dig deeper. Here are other questions that you can ask of yourself so you can feel the emotions that you need to learn. The affirmations I created will help you create a positive mindset, but perhaps it would be more meaningful to create your own affirmations. It's very simple. Start with these:

- What is the bigger force that drives me?
- What is the passion that drives me forward?
- What is my inspiration that drives me forward?
- What is my intuition telling me?
- What inspires me to move forward?
- What is my burning desire that I want to manifest?
- What is my bigger reason that drives me forward?
- What is my purpose that burns so deep inside of me?
- How can I allow my true intuition into my heart?
- How does my mindset match with my purpose?
- Is my mindset moving me forward with my purpose?
- What is the abundance that I desire that moves me forward?
- What does abundance mean to me, and how will it keep me focused on my passion?
- How is my pain driving me closer to abundance?
- What is my pain teaching me about my goal?

- What is my true inspiration?
- How can I be more of me?
- How can I connect with my heart?
- How can I step into my true power?
- Where am I hurting?
- What am I experiencing?
- What am I feeling?
- What am I not trusting?
- Where am I not trusting myself?
- What am I not allowing?
- What am I allowing?
- What am I *not* willing to receive?
- What is preventing me from receiving it?
- How can I be a better receiver?
- How do I become more of who I am?
- What am I here to receive?
- What are the stories I tell myself?
- How do I experience every moment?
- When do I stop learning?
- Where am I hurting?
- What questions do I need to ask myself?
- What questions have I not asked myself?
- What am I ready to learn next?

WEEK 1

– EMPOWERMENT

I'm here to take care of me. Only I can take care of me. It's time to trust myself. My power and my energy come from within me. I don't need to worry about the future. I am centered in my physical body. My confidence comes from my heart. This is a good reminder that I can trust myself and I can handle anything that comes my way. I am connected to my body. My true inner wisdom comes from my heart. I am grounded in my body. I am learning. I am healing. I am authentic. It's not about anyone else. It's about me and I'm empowered. I can't handle negativity. Feeling this emotion is my strength.

What am I here to learn? I need to trust where I am today. My loving inner presence is my greatest power. I am strong. I am smart. I have an abundance mindset. I am grateful. I have an open mind. I have an open heart. I trust in God's heavenly plan for happiness. God's plan is my happiness and I embrace that. The Holy Spirit enlightens me and fills my heart. I do what I need to do.

– FEELING

Life is good. Fake it until you make it, they say. My confidence comes from my heart. I can only be myself. I have boundaries. I trust in God's heavenly plan. I don't have a plan. I don't have an agenda. I can only trust in God's plan. I believe in heavenly peace and happiness. My power is in my heart. My focus is taking care of me and taking care of my feelings. I trust in God's heavenly plan for happiness and joy. My heart is open. I am healing. I honor my heart. I am empowered.

My true power is in my heart. I experience life through my heart. I trust my feelings. I am of a high value. I am joyful. I am radiant. My power is my energy. I am magnetic. I am magical. I am authentic. Jesus is with me. I trust in God's heavenly plan. My heart is my guide. My heart is open. I think deeply. I trust my inner wisdom. Why does my heart hurt so much? I want to cry. I honor myself. I am healing. If I keep making myself vulnerable, what will happen? Can I keep pretending I'm happy and that my life is amazing. People like me. People remember me. I am a good person. I love who I am. I love who I'm becoming. I am grace. I am radiance. I love myself. I give myself permission to love myself. I give myself permission to receive love. I am positive. I let go of all negativity for good. I am unconditional love and happiness.

– RECEIVE

I honor myself. My value comes from my heart. I protect my heart. I am valuable. I am secure with who I am. My heart is open. My beauty is my inner wisdom. I expect abundance, dignity, and honor. I am an elevated woman. My true power allows me to attract what I deserve. I trust in God's heavenly plan. I am grateful for finding a new way of thinking. I feel through my heart. I am getting out of my head and am focusing on my body's sensations. I have no expectations. I am healing myself. I am my own strength. Responding is my strength. Receiving is a feminine energy. I don't need to prove myself. I am worthy. I am a receiver. I am open to receiving. I am a valuable woman. I believe in my value. My heart is loving. I don't deserve abandonment. I deserve to be honored. I am worthy because I am me. The Holy Spirit lights me up and keeps me young. I deserve happiness and joy. I deserve abundance, and prosperity. I enjoy each and every moment. I stay in the moment.

– ALLOW

I am at peace. I will trust and allow. I will trust. I feel good. I am ready to let go and trust in God's heavenly plan. *My life is fuller when I allow life to happen.* I am magnetic. I attract good things. I attract abundance. I am open to whatever comes up next. I am done being controlling. Everything is okay. Everything is a lesson. I am here to learn how to be successful. I am full of love. I am full of joy. I am what I feel on the inside. I am grateful. I am at peace. I am what I think. I am positive. I am love. I embody love. I embody happiness. It's time for me to trust. I am worthy of everything that comes my way. I'm of a high value. I am filled with the Holy Spirit. What a blessing that is! I surrender to God's plan. I am ready to grow and learn every single day.

– RECEIVE

I am happy. I am inspired. I deserve happiness. My confidence comes from my heart. I deserve to receive good things. I deserve abundance. I am worthy of receiving good things. I am worthy of receiving abundance. My true power comes from my heart. My heart is beautiful. My heart is my valuable. I am very valuable. I am very powerful. I receive good energy simply because of who I am. I am grateful for who I am and where I am. I am grateful for the wisdom I am receiving. My heart is open. I am present in every moment. I am open to receiving. I am able to receive. I am valuable. I am a high-value woman. My value comes from my heart. I see myself as a beautiful person. My worth and true value comes from my heart. I see myself as a beautiful person. My worth and true value comes from within me. I am able to receive what I truly deserve. I deserve good things. I deserve abundance and happiness. I take care of me. I receive the Holy Spirit in my heart. I am committed to taking care of me. I trust in God's heavenly plan.

WEEK 2

– EMPOWERMENT

I deserve to feel my feminine energy. My first priority is my power. My power comes from my heart. I feel my power in my body. I am radiating my truth. My life is full of pleasure. Feeling good keeps me in alignment. I am centered. I am discovering the beauty within my body. My softness is my beauty. I only surround myself with things that make me feel good. I am healing and regenerating. I am naturally magnetic.

I trust in God's heavenly plan. I know there are more happy moments in heaven—more than I can imagine. I am a beautiful source of energy here on earth. I am healing. I am full of warm love. My gift to myself and others is enjoying and experiencing the moment. My power is in my energy. My power is centered inside of my body. I trust myself. I am feeling confident. I am staying connected to my inner body and my inner wisdom. I am grounded in my body. I am aligned with myself. I am inspired by my energy. I deserve happiness. I deserve abundance. I am worthy.

My happiness comes from within my heart. Stepping into my body is my true power. I listen to my body and feel my energy. I feel my sensations and notice them with grace. This is my truth. I deserve abundance. The Holy Spirit fills me up. My energy is filled up with the Holy Spirit.

I am learning to be a more loving human being. I choose to love myself. I want responsibility for my own feelings.

– FEEL

I was really angry yesterday. I had bad energy because I felt frustrated. I was experiencing loneliness, and I was afraid. My feelings showed me something was wrong. I'm sorry I lost my cool. But I'm tired of apologizing for things that are not my fault. I can take a step back and re-evaluate what happened. Even though my energy was negative, I still can learn something from what happened. I'm not afraid of being me. I know everything is going to be all right. My feelings are my power. My anger helped me bring up the emotions I needed. I will be patient. I will trust God's heavenly plan. I will trust this is part of my journey, and I am becoming a better and stronger person. I am smart. I am positive. I have an abundance mindset. I honor myself. I honor my heart. I deserve respect. I deserve abundance. I am radiant. I am filled with the Holy Spirit and happy positive feelings.

– TRUST

I thought I had this figured out. I still have more to learn. It's painful. I'm healing. My true value comes from my heart. I am vulnerable, and

I'm learning to step into my power. I trust in God's plan and in God's timing. My heart is open, and I'm full of love. I trust everything is always working out for me. I trust that this journey is making me a stronger person. I was waiting for the next learning moment—and it's here. I need to keep trusting. I can turn my pain into strength. I am smart. I am patient. I don't need a deadline. I am open. My focus is my success. My commitment is my success. My true power comes from my heart. I attract the right people. I trust me. I am committed to me. I protect my heart. I am grateful for my friendships. I have become a better person. I am not the same person. I am a better person. I deserve better. I am committed to taking care of me. I am full of love and happiness. The Holy Spirit shines through me, and I'm magnetic. I embrace this pain and trust that good will come, and it will be better than I can imagine.

– ACCEPTANCE

I trust in God's heavenly plan. I trust my heart. I trust my feminine energy. I am magnetic energy. I am learning. Things are working out the way they are meant to be. Life is happening the way it's supposed to. I am a receiver. Everything is going to be okay. I am full of joy and love. I am abundance. I expect good things. I allow good things. I am worth everything that comes my way. I am worthy of happiness and joy. I am committed to me. I take care of me. I am radiant. I am healthy. My skin is radiant. My hair is gorgeous.

My focus is me. I am anchored in me. The Holy Spirit fills my heart. My heart is open. I trust in God's heavenly plan. God has more planned for me than I can ever imagine. I am smart. I am worthy. I am a good friend. I accept who I am and where I am. I am experiencing abundance.

My greatest power is my positive mindset. I feel the positivity in my body. I am magnetic. I am magical. I am abundance. I deserve abundance. I am joy, health wealth, and abundance. I accept simply by being the soft feminine being God created. I am grateful.

– RECEIVE

I am happy. I am inspired. I deserve happiness. My confidence comes from my heart. I deserve to receive good things. I deserve abundance. I am worthy of receiving good things. I am worthy of receiving abundance. My true power comes from my heart. My heart is beautiful. My heart is valuable. I am very valuable. I am very powerful. I receive good energy simply because of who I am. I am grateful for who I am and where I am. I am grateful for the wisdom I am receiving. My heart is open. I am present in every moment. I am open to receiving. I am able to receive. I am valuable. I am a high-value woman. My value comes from my heart. I see myself as a beautiful person. My worth and true value comes from my heart. I see myself as a beautiful person. My worth and true value comes from within me. I am able to receive what I truly deserve. I deserve good things. I deserve abundance and happiness. I take care of me. I receive the Holy Spirit in my heart. I am committed to taking care of me. I trust in God's heavenly plan.

WEEK 3

– EMPOWERMENT

I am grateful. I am here for me. I am a receiver. I deserve abundance. My heart is full. I am attracting everything I want in my life. I am magnetic. My true value is anchored in my heart and my body. I am here to experience the moment. I trust in God's heavenly plan. My heart is open. I am grounded in my feelings. I am staying connected to my physical self. I am connected to my inner wisdom. I am mesmerizing. I am radiant. My confidence comes from my heart and staying connected. My purpose is to stay connected to my heart. I surrender to my purpose.

My true power comes from when I slow down each moment. I live inside every moment. I am a high-quality woman. I am open to receiving. I'm okay. I'm open to trusting and receiving what I've been given. I deserve kindness and love. I am excited to be attracting abundance. I trust in God's plan. I am filled with the Holy Spirit.

– FEEL

I am empowered to feel my feelings. My true power comes from my deeper feelings. What am I here to learn? I am experiencing my own life. My feelings are my guide. I surrender to my emotions and my feelings. I trust myself. I trust my intuition. I surrender to my energy. I am dynamic. I am attractive. I am authentic. My heart is open. I am connecting to my heart. All of my attention belongs to me. Abundance flows easily and effortlessly to me every single day. I am healing. What is my vulnerability? What is my pain? What are my deeper feelings? I'm afraid. I'm always afraid. I need to trust in God's heavenly plan. The Holy Spirit fills my heart. I honor the spirit that lives in me. I honor myself. I honor God's beauty. I am amazed at God's beauty.

What am I here to learn? I am happy. I am blessed. I am content. I am listening. My story is my story. I am here to learn. I am here for me. I am here to learn. I am here for me. I am here to grow. My purpose is to stay connected to my heart. I trust in God's great plan and know things will work out better than I can ever imagine. I am excited to be creating abundance in my life. I am magnetic energy. I am valuable. I deserve abundance. I am worthy.

– TRUST

I have trust issues.

What am I here to learn? I trust in God's heavenly plan for happiness. My past experiences do not create my future. I can handle everything that comes my way. My history is not my destiny. Being private doesn't serve me. Everything is always working out for me. I am not a broken shell. I am doing this work to build my inner trust. My power is in my heart. Where do I not trust myself? Abundance flows easily and effortlessly to me every single day. I am committed to myself. I am committed to keeping a journal and meditating every single day. I am learning to be more trusting in myself. I radiate soft, feminine energy. I have nothing to hide. I cherish myself. I am good enough. My heart is open. My heart is filled with love, joy, and happiness. My vulnerability is my strength. Trusting is my strength. Jesus is my guide. My heart is my purpose. I surrender to my purpose. I am so grateful. I will trust the signs. My strength comes from facing my deeper fears. My pain makes me stronger every day. I need to learn to love myself.

– ACCEPTANCE

What questions do I need to ask myself? It's time to stop the worry. It's time to allow in what I'm here to learn. I can't worry. I can only allow. I trust in God's heavenly plan for love and joy. I deserve abundance. I expect to be treated with respect. I am radiant. I expect abundance. I expect happiness. The Holy Spirit fills my heart, and I radiate that love and light. I'm in love with life. I am positive. I am strong, feminine energy. I attract abundance. I am so grateful for life. I'm grateful for my family and all the love that surrounds me.

– RECEIVE

I am a receiver. I am a receiver of good energy. My heart is open, and I'm full of happiness. I am anchored in my heart. My heart is my most valuable asset. My true worth is my value. My purpose is to stay connected to my heart. I surrender to my purpose. I am capable of receiving good things. I am worthy of receiving abundance. Abundance is flowing into my life every day. I am excited to be creating abundance. I deserve abundance. My heart deserves abundance. Good things come to me naturally. I am magnetic energy. The Holy Spirit fills my soul.

WEEK 4

– EMPOWERMENT

My heart is full of love. I am grateful for this journey. My energy is my strength. I'm okay. My energy is good. I'm full of love, joy, and happiness. I have a lot to work on. I'm experiencing loneliness. It does hurt, but it's making me stronger. I trust in God's heavenly plan. My feelings are telling me everything is going to be okay. Everything will be okay. I don't have to have a plan.

My purpose is staying connected to my heart. I am dynamic feminine energy. I am authentic. I am open. I only attract high energy people. I'm okay. My energy is soft, sacred feminine energy. I see the signs. The signs are my reminder to trust. I don't understand. I don't need to know.

What am I here to learn? I want happiness. I am who I am, and this my strength. I am full of patience. I am dynamic. I am radiant. Abundance flows to me.

– FEEL

I've been stifling myself because I've been afraid. I deserve better. My feelings are my guide. My heart is open. I am not afraid of any emotions. My feelings are a power place. I am so grateful. I am so grateful to have found my heart. I need to stay connected to my heart. I need to stay connected to me. My purpose is staying connected to my heart. I raise my energy. I raise my vibration. I do deserve abundance. I do know what needs to be done. I can make this work. I am confident. I am an action taker. My heart is love. I am a good person. I am a good friend. I give love and receive love freely. I am smart. I have courage. I am amazing. I have amazing strength and energy. I attract good energy. Abundance flows to me easily and effortlessly every day. I trust in God's heavenly plan for happiness. I am strength. I am excited to be building my abundance in my life. I have the courage to do it.

– TRUST

I am grounded in my feminine energy. It's time for me to clean up my life. There's a reason for all of this happening. It is truly time for me to step up. I can't let any of my pain be in vain. I'm tired of being below average. I am ready to receive. Everything is always working out for me. Everything is okay. I'm being taken care of. I'm dynamic. I'm regenerating. I meditate love, joy, and happiness. I trust in God's heavenly plan. I am at peace with where I am. Now is the time to embrace this place. I am what I think. I am a magnet for positive things to attract towards me. I don't need anyone to make me happy. I make myself happy. I make myself happy by making others happy. I deserve happiness, love, and joy.

I am worthy of abundance. I am vibrant. I am afraid, and that's okay. I am here for me. And I have no expectations. I'm here to learn. I embrace life. I protect my heart. I am full of grace. I am sacred feminine energy and softness. Trusting gives me space to observe. Trusting is about managing my emotional investment. Trusting is an energy. Trusting is a relaxed energy that allows me to radiate my natural worth. Trusting is creating and embracing space. It's something that a woman with a full life does naturally.

– ACCEPTANCE

I am feminine energy. I am filled with the Holy Spirit. I am filled with abundance. My purpose is to stay connected to my heart. I am grateful for this journey. I am learning that I can choose to play small or open my heart to abundance.

What am I here to learn? I am a blessing. I am a blessing to others. I love being myself. I am happiness. I trust in God's heavenly plan. I am excited to create abundance. I feel it. *How will it feel when abundance arrives?*

– RECEIVE

I am a receiver. I receive good energy. My heart is full. I am worthy of receiving the energy of building abundance. My true power is in my heart. My energy is beautiful and valuable. I am very powerful. My commitment is to me. This is who I am. I am worthy. I am valuable. I allow only good energy into me and into my heart. My true power as a woman is my full presence. My magnetic energy comes from trusting. I am alive, and I am full of energy. I embrace my love. I am a high-value woman. My core power is anchored in my true value. My true value comes from within me. I experience every moment through good energy. I deserve happiness. I deserve abundance. I am worthy of great things. I make myself feel good. I trust in God's heavenly plan.

WEEK 5

– EMPOWERMENT

I am soft, sacred energy, and I deserve abundance. My heart is filled with love, joy, and happiness. I am worthy. My soft, sacred energy is my magnetic power. My confidence comes from staying connected to my heart. Trusting is my true energy. I'm grateful for my journey. Abundance flows to me easily and effortlessly every single day. My inner child deserves my love.

What am I here to learn? I trust in God's heavenly plan. The Holy Spirit fills my heart. The Holy Spirit helps me feel my energy. I am sacred elegance. I am divine energy. Everything is working out the way they're meant to be. I trust this journey. I'm grateful. I will trust. I am quiet feminine energy. Everything naturally comes to me with ease and grace. I am experiencing every present moment fully. I am a gift.

– FEEL

My heart is full. My heart is lit up by a ball of fire. This ball of fire fills my body. My body is full of warmth. This warmth is love. I feel the love in my heart and throughout my body. My energy is warmth. Others can feel my warmth. Others can feel my positive energy. I am full of life. I am full of color. I am vibrant. I am radiant. I feel love and peace inside of my body. I only feel the sensation of love in my heart. My heart is an overflowing source of love. My purpose is to stay connected to my heart. My heart is full of abundant love.

Love is the fire that lives in me through the Holy Spirit. This ball of fire is my source of abundance. I am creating this source. The Holy Spirit is burning inside of me. I only know love. I am creating abundance. I surround myself with good energy. I am finding me. I am taking care of me. I have good intuition. I understand people. I am light. I am love. I am full. My heart is joyful. I am creating. The Holy Spirit is driving me. I see the signs for me to trust. I am listening to those signs to trust.

My masculine energy is saying this to me. I need to respect those signs. I don't play games. I live. I trust myself.

– TRUST

I am trusting. I am grateful for this journey. I'm here for me.

What am I here to learn? My true value is my energy. I am a deeper soul. Everything is always working out for me. There must be value in this. I trust my intuition. My vulnerability is my authenticity. I will trust. My heart is open. My true power is my intuition. I show up for myself. I take care of myself. I take care of my heart. I am here for me. Only I can be here for me. My inner child needs to trust me. I trust in God's heavenly plan. I'm here to observe my behavior.

My vulnerability is my shield. My vulnerability is my gift to the world. My power is not in protecting myself. Sharing my vulnerability is my gift to others. My feminine energy is my truth. My energy is soft and sacred. I am fully present with love, joy, and happiness. The Holy Spirit fills my heart and gives me strength. I accept God's plan. I am worthy of abundance. My purpose is staying connected to my heart. I surrender to my purpose. Trusting is my strength.

– ACCEPTANCE

God has a plan for me. I am learning. I am healing. My feminine energy is my strength. I trust in God's heavenly plan. I am here to learn. My purpose is my connection to my heart. I soften and surrender to my purpose. I trust I am on the right path. Abundance flows to me easily and effortlessly every day. My belief system comes from what I believe and feel in my body. My energy is very full. I am resourcing energy. I am regenerating love and joy. I feel only good sensations. I am attracting good energy. I am attracting the energy I have and feel inside of me. I make peace with where I am. It is my loving responsibility to take care of me. My positive body state is my magnetic energy. I am full of happiness, and I am secure with my happiness. I create my positive energy. I deserve abundance. I am blessed to receive the Holy Spirit's love inside me. It is my loving responsibility to accept myself. I am excited to be on this journey. I deserve abundance. My true power is my magnetic energy.

– RECEIVE

I am worthy of receiving only energy that values me. I am the holder of beautiful, valuable energy. I am a receiver. I practice receiving. I don't need to do anything to be valuable. My confidence and self-worth come from my vibration. My vibration is my energy, which is created by my heart. I am a good receiver. I am getting comfortable receiving. I am comfortable being a high-value woman. I have a loving heart. I am a beautiful person. I am worthy of love and happiness. I trust in God's heavenly plan. I am anchored in my faith. I am worthy. My goal is financial freedom. I am worthy of receiving love and abundance. Money flows to me easily and effortlessly every day. I am the source of everything I desire. I am vulnerable to what I receive. The Holy Spirit fills my body with love and happiness with every breath. I am grace. I am a magnetic center. My positive energy flows back to others. I naturally radiate love and happiness with every breath. I am grace. I am soft. I am vulnerable.

WEEK 6

– EMPOWERMENT

I am more compassionate with myself and others. I want joy and happiness in my heart.

What am I here to learn? I don't want to suffer. I need the Holy Spirit to fill me up with positive loving energy. I love myself. I give myself permission to give love and receive love freely. My strength is my feminine energy. I am experiencing pain. I've created this myself. My heart is my strength. I am here to surrender to my heart. I'm the only one that I can trust. It doesn't matter what anyone else thinks. I love myself. Staying grounded in my body is my strength. It's okay to feel this pain. It's good for me to experience the hurt. I am experiencing pain and hurt, and I truly feel it.

What am I here to learn? I'm here to get inside of every moment. I'm the only one who can help myself. I am soft, sacred feminine energy. That is my truth.

– FEEL

I am grateful for the day. I am experiencing hurt right now.

What am I here to learn? My feelings are my best friends. I don't need a solution. My heart is open. I miss the feeling of joy and love. I am afraid of expressing who I really am. I am afraid. I feel shame. My confidence comes from my heart. It hurts so much. I need to deal with my wounds. I want happiness. I want joy. I honor myself. I honor my heart. I am worthy of love. I am worthy of abundance. Abundance flows to me easily and effortlessly every day. The only person that matters is my inner child. My inner child needs to be heard. The Holy Spirit fills my heart with joy, love, and happiness. It is my job to feel these emotions. My purpose is staying connected to my heart. I surrender to my heart and my purpose. I am committed to taking care of myself and filling my heart with love.

– TRUST

I want love in my heart. I am committed to me. I am here every day to take care of my heart. I didn't trust myself. Everything is okay. My true value is staying connected to myself. My heart is open. Everything is always working out for me.

What am I here to learn? My intuition tells me that I'm loved and that I can trust. My pain is my strength. My confidence comes from my heart. I am committed to showing up for myself. I trust in God's heavenly plan for happiness. What is this teaching me?

What am I here to learn? I am soft, sacred feminine energy. I radiate love, joy, and happiness. My body radiates this. My skin radiates this. I am a beautiful warm glowing light that others are attracted to. My gentleness and vulnerability are my strength. I deserve to receive everything I desire.

I deserve abundance. I am worthy. My sensitivity *is* my gift to the world. My power is not in protecting myself. My soft, sacred feminine energy is my truth. My positive energy attracts positive energy. I have compassion for myself. I am grateful the Holy Spirit has compassion for me. I trust God's heavenly plan. Trusting is my strength.

– ACCEPTANCE

Life is fun. Life is an adventure. I am open to life. I deserve abundance. I am worthy of fun. My energy is my confidence. I am listening. I am grateful that the Holy Spirit fills my heart. I am attracting good energy. Everything is falling into place for me. Everything is okay. I am learning new lessons every day. I am healing. I am creating. I am filled with love and joy from the Holy Spirit. I trust myself. I am committed to myself. I am making peace with every moment. I am what I think. I am confident. I am joy. I don't want to judge. I attract only love and happiness. My heart is open. I am grateful for my heart. I am grateful for my loving heart. I am grateful to know I am a forgiven child of God and to know the Holy Spirit lives in me. I follow my heart. I know my purpose is to stay connected to my heart. I love myself. I protect my heart. I have patience. I trust in God's heavenly plan. I trust that the joy in heaven is something I can't understand here. I will trust God's timing.

– RECEIVE

I am a receiver. I am a gracious receiver. I am worthy of receiving. The Holy Spirit fills me up. I am valuable. I am radiant. My energy is beautiful and valuable. I am open to receiving. Life makes me happy. I am experiencing giving and receiving. My power is to experience receiving. I am capable of receiving. I am listening. I am becoming comfortable receiving. I am valuable. I believe in my value. My purpose is staying connected to my loving heart. My worth and confidence comes from my heart. I am grateful for this journey. The Holy Spirit helps me heal and create. I am worthy of healing and creating. I am worthy of receiving these two gifts from the Holy Spirit. I trust in God's heavenly plan for happiness. I am grateful for this journey. I am stronger. I have hope. I am trusting. I am empowered to trust. I trust good things will come and things will be better than I can ever imagine. I will trust God. I am grateful for this journey. I surrender to God's plan. I am free, wild, and spontaneous energy. My feminine energy is my confidence.

WEEK 7

– EMPOWERMENT

Who am I?

What am I here to learn? My truth is that I am sacred energy. I am soft, sacred energy. My value is my energy. I trust in God's heavenly plan. I can't create anything better. I am here to expand myself. What am I here to surrender to? My value is not in my perfection. My soft, sacred energy is my strength. My vulnerability is my strength. I surrender to God's heavenly plan.

What am I afraid of? Am I afraid of embarrassment? I want happiness. I just want love, joy, and happiness. What is my identity? Who am I? I surrender to everything unknown. I surrender to being led by God. This is my courage. Letting go is my courage. I am being shown how to feel safe and secure. My brain needs to shut off, and it's time to feel confidence from my heart and soul. My power and energy lie in my body. I am centered in my body.

Trusting is my confidence. I am attracting everything I need in life. I am pulling the whole world to me. My feminine energy is my strength. My empowered life comes from connecting inside of me. I can experience the world from my true feminine center. This is my true power. I'm here to experience every moment and every pain. My pain is my strength. My pain makes my magnetic field stronger. My loving presence is my greatest gift. My inner feminine energy is my gift to others.

– FEEL

My heart is my confidence. My feelings are my power place.

What am I here to learn? My feelings are my best friends. My feelings are my guide. My heart is full of love, joy, and happiness. I radiate good energy. I am authentic. I only attract good energy. I am who I am. I am enjoying the journey. My life is a blessing. Only good energy flows through me. My heart is magnetic energy. This is my power. I honor myself. I honor my inner child. I am soft and warm. I experience joy. I have no agenda. My feminine energy is authentic.

Trusting is my power. I'm keeping my energy open. I am comfortable with myself. My pleasure is in the present moment. I am grateful for every moment. I have no expectations. My focus is on my business. My heart is grateful. I am magnetic feminine energy. I trust my intuition. I am worthy of abundance. Trusting is my strength. I am lovable the way I am. I am worthy of good energy. I am loveable. I am a powerful, magnetizing woman. Abundance flows to me easily and effortlessly every day.

– TRUST

I love myself. I honor myself. I have beautiful energy. I trust myself. I trust in God's heavenly plan. I am here for me. I am learning from this experience. My power is my energy. I am here to build my confidence. I trust everything is always working out for me. My pain is my strength. Making myself vulnerable is my strength. My purpose is staying connected to my heart. I surrender to my purpose. I am holding space for myself. I am devoted to myself. Where do I not trust myself?

What am I here to learn? I am soft, sacred feminine energy. I attract only high-level relationships. I am committed to myself. I am the only one who can take care of me in the way I truly want. I love myself. I give myself permission to give love and receive love freely. I am dynamic. I radiate love, joy, and happiness. I cherish myself. I am grateful for this gift of finding myself. My heart is open. Only I can give myself the love I truly desire. God has a plan, and I trust in God's plan. I am magnetic energy. Only good and abundant energy flows to me. I am here to love and respect myself. Everything is okay. Everything is working out the way it's supposed to. I love myself. My feminine energy is my strength.

– ACCEPTANCE

I trust in God's heavenly plan for happiness. My dream life will happen. The gift of allowing is receiving from the Holy Spirit. I am grateful for this journey. I am attracting what I want towards me. Everything is always working out for me. Everything is okay. I am learning. I am regenerating love, joy, and happiness. I am soft, feminine energy. I am fullness. I am growing. I am here to take care of me. My energy attracts everything I desire. God's plan for happiness for me is above and beyond better than anything I can ever imagine. I deserve abundance. I am worthy of abundance. I feel the energy of abundance coming to me. I feel it. It feels good. I have no control over what it will be like or how it will happen. I know it will. I am open to receiving. I know the Holy Spirit fills me up. Jesus holds my hand. My loving energy attracts abundance in ways I can't predict or create on my own. My heart is open to God's plan. I am centered and grounded in my faith. I'm a forgiven child of God. I am loved.

– RECEIVE

I am valuable energy. I am worthy of receiving only good energy. I've learned that my true value and my true confidence is my valuable energy. When I trust, I am receiving energy. I don't need to prove my energy to anyone. I am worthy of love, happiness, and good things. I am worthy of receiving good energy. I am a good receiver. My true power is being fully present by embracing my own energy. The Holy Spirit gives me that joy. I am filled with joy and peace. I am very valuable. I believe in my value. My nature is my loving heart. I am learning. I am healing. I am building abundance in my life. Abundance flows to me easily and effortlessly every day. I trust in God's heavenly plan for happiness.

WEEK 8

– EMPOWERMENT

I am who I am. I am unique, and that's what makes me beautiful. My purpose is staying connected to my heart. I am soft, sacred feminine energy. No one can make me feel bad because I love myself in a way no one would ever understand. I love myself, and that's all that matters. I don't need love from anywhere else. I am a goddess and the Holy Spirit fills my heart over and over. I love myself. I make myself feel safe and secure. I deserve honor. I am an elevated goddess.

I am worthy of abundance. I honor myself. I am always at my very best. I embrace where I am. I embrace me. I am a powerful, dynamic woman. I am a mountain on the inside. I am receiver of good energy. I am fully present to my own energy. I am fully present to my vulnerability and my feminine energy. I protect myself. I deserve respect. Trusting is my strength. I trust in God's heavenly plan. It's not up to me to create anything.

– FEEL

Yesterday was a really tough day. I am the creator of my happiness. My vibration and my energy are my strength. I'm not here to solve anyone else's problems. I am a beautiful person. I radiate joy, love, and happiness. Abundance flows to me easily and effortlessly every single day.

What am I here to learn? Living small doesn't serve me. I am open to learning. I am dynamic. I am magnetic. I am authentic. I only attract good energy. My feelings are a power place. I'm scared out of my mind. Fear is making me move forward. I am a queen. I am a goddess. I am an elevated woman. I am normal. I am responsible for my actions. My power comes from trusting. I trust in God's heavenly plan.

– TRUST

I am here for me. I trust everything is working out. I trust in God's heavenly plan. I am here for me. I have been brought on this journey for a purpose. I trust this journey. The pain has nothing to do with my value and my worth. I am learning from this pain. I am grounded in who I am. My worthiness comes from me and not any other person. I trust in the future. Whatever lies in front of me I can trust. I am becoming a deeper soul and a deeper woman. Whatever comes my way I can handle. I have more and more self-trust every day. I am soft, sacred feminine energy. I trust in life and that everything is always working out for me. There must be value in this. I am learning from this experience. I am ready to learn from this pain. My history is not my destiny.

My true power is feeling my pain, and trusting things are always working out for me. I am here for me. I am here for my self-confidence. I have to trust my boundaries. My vulnerability is my strength. I am a warm, loving, beautiful woman. I surrender to trusting myself. I trust everything is working out for me. I am dynamic. I am radiant. Where do I not trust myself? I attract everything I want in life. I surrender to my purpose. My purpose is staying connected to my heart. As I become more trusting in myself, others can trust me. My positive energy is my strength. My confidence comes from this feminine energy.

– ACCEPTANCE

Nothing makes sense to me. My brain is on overload. My strength comes from trusting. I trust in God's plan for heavenly happiness. Staying connected to my heart, and showing love to others, is my purpose. God has a bigger and better plan for me, and I am here to surrender to my purpose. Everything is working out the way it's supposed to. I don't create. Trusting is my strength. I'm grateful for this journey. My energy is my strength. I surrender to God's heavenly plan. I'm not feeling aligned. *Feminine energy is about receiving and allowing.* Things are enfolding the way they are supposed to. Everything is okay. I am growing. I am full, dynamic energy regenerating love, joy, and happiness over and over again. I need to be at peace with where I am. I am choosing abundance. I am worthy of everything I desire. Everything I want comes from within me. I am the creator of everything I desire. God's plan is my destination. I humbly bow to receiving God's heavenly plan. My life is not my plan. I am here to receive. I am worthy of receiving abundance.

– RECEIVE

I'm afraid. What am I telling myself? Facing my fears is healing. I am on a journey of finding my purpose. My purpose is staying connected to my heart. My power is my heart. I am soft, feminine energy. I can handle with grace anything that's coming my way. I am learning to be grounded in my body.

What am I here to learn? My energy is my power. My confidence comes from my heart. I am connecting with myself. My power comes from experiencing the moment. My EMPOWERMENTs have created this journey. My past is not my destiny. My loving presence is my beauty. My looks don't define me. My heart defines me. I am positive energy. My heart is full of love, joy, and happiness. I trust in God's heavenly plan for true happiness.

WEEK 9

– EMPOWERMENT

My confidence comes from my feminine energy. I am experiencing pain, and I surrender to it. My confidence and steadiness come from experiencing this pain. I trust myself. I can handle anything that comes my way. I am connected to my true inner wisdom. I am grounded in myself. My feminine energy needs my attention. I am soft, sacred feminine energy. My true power is experiencing the moment and getting inside of every moment. My power is feeling all the sensations in my body and my heart. Feeling this pain makes me stronger. I love myself. I trust in God's heavenly plan for happiness. Everything is always working out for me. God has a plan, and I'm here to trust in it. I surrender to my purpose. My purpose is staying connected to my heart.

What am I here to learn? I am here to play in the moment. I am enjoying the process. I know my value. All I need to do is be myself. I feel good about myself. I am amazing and magnetic. I light myself up from the inside. I love myself. Only I can make myself feel safe and secure. I take care of my heart. All I have is trust.

What am I here to learn? My intuition says to trust God's heavenly plan. Everything is always working out for me. God's plan of abundance for me is better than I can ever imagine. My job as a feminine energy is to trust that everything is working out.

– FEEL

God is love. I am love. I am here for myself. My value is my energy. I am trustworthy. I trust in God's heavenly plan. Trusting is the hardest thing I've ever done. Trusting is my strength. I believe in the signs. It's my job to take care of myself. Everything is always working out for me. My heart is open. My masculine energy makes me stronger. I trust in God's heavenly plan. Everything is good. My success is my destiny. My vulnerability is my strength.

What am I here to learn? I need to stay out of my head. My strength is my body. My feelings are my intuition. I am soft, sacred feminine energy. My pain is my strength. I am not in charge. God is in charge, and has a plan. I trust in God's heavenly plan for true happiness. My heart is full. My heart is love. My purpose is staying connected to my heart. I surrender to my heart, my purpose, and my softness, and to staying sacred.

– TRUST

Everything is working out for me. My pain makes me a deeper soul. My heart is magnetic. There is value in my pain. Vulnerability is my strength. Trusting my vulnerability is my strength. I trust my vulnerability. My heart is open. Where do I not trust myself? I attract only high-level authentic energy. I trust myself. I am committed to me. I take care of myself. I honor my heart. I am soft, sacred feminine energy on the inside out. Trust is my strength. My energy is my strength. I am connected to my heart. I surrender to that purpose. Observing my breath is my strength. I deserve love and to be loved. Love is my power. I radiate love.

The Holy Spirit fills my heart and body with love. My heart deserves my full attention and undivided love. Gentleness and vulnerability are my shield. It's my right to receive everything I desire. The Holy Spirit fills me up with warmth and love. My energy is my true power. My sensitivity is my gift to the world. My power is not in protecting myself. My softness and gentleness are a gift. I cherish myself and my energy. My feminine energy is my truth. I surrender to my purpose. My purpose is staying connected to my heart. Only I can give myself the happiness I truly desire. I trust in God's heavenly plan. Everything I desire is coming my way. My heart is open, and I am ready to receive love, joy, and abundance.

– ACCEPTANCE

I am able to receive energy from uplifting sources. I value myself as a beautiful person. I am worthy of receiving spirited sacred energy. I am ready to receive radiance. I am ready to receive abundance. I am worthy. I am ready to receive life. I trust in God's heavenly plan for happiness.

What am I here to learn? I am filled with the Holy Spirit. I am a forgiven child of God. There are so many sources for good energy ready for me. I am love. I am worthy of love. Love is everywhere. My heart is open. My heart is open to receiving abundance and positive love from every living thing. I am worthy. I am grateful for this journey.

What am I here to learn? My pain is my strength. Trusting is the answer. Trusting is hard for me. My energy is amazing. I am worthy of loving friendships. Trusting helps me protect my heart. Trust is a loving act to myself. I am good energy. I am love. I give myself permission to be happy. My power lies in my ability to receive. I am attracting everything I desire. I naturally radiate love, joy, and happiness with every breath. I radiate this amazing energy. I radiate from the inside out. I have access to this amazing energy. This is who I really am.

– RECEIVE

I am a receiver of good energy. I deserve abundance. I am valuable for who I am. I am soft, feminine energy. I am a gift to others. I am magnetic energy. Others are attracted to my powerful center. My feminine energy is valuable. Everything is working out the way it's meant to be. I am worthy of what's happening. My discipline protects me. I'm not waiting. I am receiving. I am present in this journey. I feel this pain, but this pain makes me stronger. I trust in God's heavenly plan. I am valuable. I am an elevated woman. My value is my truth. I am worthy of good energy. I am a receiver of good energy. I am here to take care of myself. I protect myself.

Only I can love my heart the way it needs love. I love myself. I give and receive love freely. I am in control of my life. I'm the only one who can take care of me. It doesn't matter what anyone does for me. I'm the one. My value comes from the Holy Spirit. The Holy Spirit fills me up. I am radiant. I radiate love, joy, and happiness. I am a receiver of good energy. I am a receiver of abundance. I am a forgiven child of God. I'm not perfect. I am open to my vulnerability. I surrender to God's plan. My heart is love and forgiveness. I am grateful for finding my confidence. Trusting is my strength. God has a plan. I have to trust God's plan. My life is a gift from God. God wants me to cherish it and take care of me.

WEEK 10

– EMPOWERMENT

My confidence comes from my feminine energy. I am experiencing pain, and I surrender to it. My confidence and steadiness come from experiencing this pain. I trust myself. I can handle anything that comes my way. I am connected to my true inner wisdom. I am grounded in myself. My feminine energy needs my attention. I am soft, sacred feminine energy.

My true power is experiencing the moment and getting inside of every moment. My power is feeling all the sensations in my body and my heart. Feeling this pain makes me stronger. I love myself. I love me. I trust in God's heavenly plan for happiness. Everything is always working out for me. God has a plan, and I'm here to trust in it. I surrender to my purpose. My purpose is staying connected to my heart.

What am I here to learn? I am here to play in the moment. I am enjoying the process. I know my value. All I need to do is be myself. I feel good about myself. I am amazing and magnetic. I light myself up from the inside. I love myself. Only I can make myself feel safe and secure. I take care of my heart. All I have is trust.

What am I here to learn? My intuition says trust God's heavenly plan. Everything is always working out for me. God's plan of abundance for me is better than I can ever imagine. My job as a feminine energy is to trust that everything is working out.

– FEEL

I am beautiful. I radiate beauty. My heart is full of love, joy, and happy energy. I am worthy of this. I am an elevated high energy. I trust in God's heavenly plan. I am grateful. I have become a better person. I am life. I have an open heart. I have found my heart. I love myself. I give love and receive love freely.

What am I here to learn? I am healing. My purpose is staying connected to my heart. My positive energy is my power. I am authentic. I am vulnerable. My feelings are my power place. I am so afraid. I am becoming a better person. I deserve elevated relationships. Abundance is coming to me. Trusting is my true power. My tears ground me. I honor my feelings. I am soft, sacred feminine energy.

– TRUST

I'm tired. I'm so very tired. My feelings are empty today. I have compassion for me because I want solutions and resolutions. I am attached to the process and detached from the outcome. I am an elevated woman with soft, sacred energy. I am worthy of love, joy, and abundance. I clear my mind and expect nothing. I have no expectations. I know this is for me. I can only trust. Trusting is my strength. Staying out of my head and my mind is my strength. I am grateful for this experience. I trust in God's heavenly plan. I will be okay. Everything is always working out for me. I honor myself. I honor my heart. I honor my inner beauty. The Holy Spirit fills me up and gives me new life and energy over and over again. I am sacred feminine energy. I deserve abundance. I am worthy of receiving abundance.

– ACCEPTANCE

My life is full. My heart is open. I trust in God's heavenly plan for happiness. I am open to allowing good things and fun into my life. I am here to protect myself. I protect my heart. I am worthy of abundance. I am soft, sacred feminine energy. Everything is okay. This is my opportunity to grow. I am dynamic, radiant, gorgeous and beautiful energy. I deserve fullness. I am worthy of love, joy, and happiness. I am fun. Everything is working out the way it's supposed to. Abundance flows to me easily and effortlessly every single day. My life is a result of what I think of myself. I am the creator of everything I want in my life. My true power is my sacred, soft energy. I am wild, care-free energy. The Holy Spirt fills me with inspiration.

– RECEIVE

What am I here to learn? I am worthy of receiving abundance. My energy is my value. My purpose is staying connected to my heart. I am beautiful and valuable soft, sacred feminine energy. I am a good receiver. I deserve happiness. I am worthy of happiness and abundance. Trusting is my strength. I show up for me. I am committed to me. I am valuable.

My core power comes from my loving heart. My heart makes me a beautiful person. I deserve everything I desire. I am worthy of abundance and success. I am feminine energy, and I'm ready to receive. My power lies in my ability to receive. Energy moves through me as I receive the Holy Spirit. I am a magnetic center receiving abundant energy. I radiate this same energy back to the world. I naturally radiate beauty, love, and happiness. I radiate deep love, deep happiness, and deep joy. All the energy I'll ever need is within me. I am valuable. I trust in God's heavenly plan for true happiness. My plan is not the best. My plan is allowing God's plan to bring me happiness and abundance. Receiving is my strength.

WEEK 11

– EMPOWERMENT

Trusting is my strength. I love myself. I protect myself. My feminine energy is soft and sacred. My self-confidence comes from my feminine power. I attract everything I want. Everything is always working out for me. I am attracting everything I need in life. My power and confidence come from my heart and experiencing everything in my body. I trust in God's heavenly plan for happiness. The Holy Spirit fills me with energy of love, joy, and abundance.

I deserve abundance. It's my job to get involved in every single moment and experiencing where I am. I am authentic. I am vulnerable. My pain is my strength. Experiencing this pain makes me stronger. I am here to learn and to love. Love is the power of my truth. I honor the feminine goddess inside of me. I am beautiful. I am radiant. I radiate love, joy, and abundance. I will trust God's plan.

– FEEL

I have been shown how safe and secure I can feel. I trust in God's heavenly plan. I don't understand. I don't need to understand. Being honest with myself is my strength. Trusting is my strength. I am a high-value woman with soft, sacred energy. My purpose is staying connected to my heart. The Holy Spirit fills me up. Filling my heart with love is my strength. Does my fear lie to me? I am not afraid of who I am. My feelings are my power place. I will be okay. Everything will be okay. I am becoming stronger. I am healing. My pain is giving me strength. I honor myself. I honor my feelings. I am connected to myself. My connection to my heart is my purpose.

What am I here to learn? I trust in God's heavenly plan. In what way am I most likely to find my peace? God is in control. I don't control. I am not afraid to trust. My pain is giving me strength. I am afraid, and my only power is my feminine energy, which is trusting. I am divine sacred and soft energy. I trust in God's heavenly plan. I have this incredible connection with people. I am incredibly connected to myself in a way I've never been before. I deserve love, joy, happiness, and abundance. I see the signs. My strength is my energy. My value is not my perfection. I am authentic.

– TRUST

Everything is always working out for me. My emotional attachment to my feeling of pain gives me strength. Staying neutral lessens my pain.

What am I here to learn? Time heals pain. My confidence comes from my heart. How do I surrender myself? Trusting is my strength.

What am I here to learn? I am committed to me. I love myself. I give myself permission to give love and receive love freely. What am I observing? I don't know how to feel. I feel empty. The emptiness makes me sad. I'm afraid. My energy is my strength. I am soft, sacred feminine energy. I don't understand. I don't need to understand. I have to trust myself and trust in God's heavenly plan. The Holy Spirit fills my heart with love, joy, and abundance.

– ACCEPTANCE

I am soft, sacred feminine energy. My heart generates amazing abundant energy that guides me. The Holy Spirit fills me with love, joy, and happiness. It's time to protect me. I am grateful for this journey. Everything is working out the way it's supposed to. I deserve abundance. I am ready and worthy of receiving God's love for joy, happiness, and abundance.

– RECEIVE

What am I here to learn? I am soft, sacred and positive feminine energy. My heart hurts, but my pain is my strength. I trust in God's heavenly plan. God's plan is the only plan and the best plan. I am a receiver of good energy. I am attracting abundance, but I don't know how. It hurts so much not knowing God's plan. It hurts so much not taking charge. Trusting is my strength. I am worthy of receiving good energy. My gift to others is receiving good energy. I am magnetic feminine energy. My heart is magnetic. Receiving good energy is my strength. I am enough. I am worthy. I am a good receiver. I am receiving. I am open to receiving. I receive God's energy with joy. It's my job to receive. Receiving feels uncomfortable. I am a high-value woman. I believe in my high value. I am a beautiful person. I deserve high level energy. I am valuable. I am worthy because I am me. My true value is my energy that I hold in my heart. My strength comes from taking care of my heart. I forgive myself. My heart needs my love. I'm the only one who truly knows how to love myself. I am worthy of love. My heart and softness are my strength. I am ready to receive.

WEEK 12

– EMPOWERMENT

I am becoming more of who I am. My feminine energy is my strength. God has an amazing plan for me. My brain is overthinking. Why do I need to understand? Why do I need to have all the answers? Connecting to my inner wisdom is my strength. Trusting is my strength. My purpose is staying connected to my heart. My energy is love. Slowing down the tempo and the momentum helps me stay in the moment. Staying in my body and feeling my skin and feeling my sensations helps me stay grounded in my feminine energy.

My feminine energy is soft and sacred. I'm feeling confused, but I know it's because I'm going into my head. I'm living the life I desire. I'm attracting everything I want. When I become afraid, it's fear. Overthinking creates fear. I'm learning more and more about myself. Fear means I am growing on the inside. I am grateful for this journey. Connecting into myself is my greatest gift to others. I am attracting everything I desire. I love myself. I take care of my heart.

– FEEL

What am I here to learn? I'm afraid. My strength and confidence come from my heart. I'm not that strong. My energy is my strength. I am experiencing so much pain. My feelings are my guide. I'm scared. My heart is open. My power is my energy. I'm authentic. I only want to attract those with the same energy. My feelings come from a place of power—and not a place of shame. Why am I afraid? I love myself. I give myself permission to give love and receive love freely. What am I feeling? I'm feeling fear. This is my power. I am afraid. I am so afraid. My energy is my beauty. I honor my soft, sacred feminine energy. I am beautiful. I am radiant. I deserve abundance. I am worthy of love, joy, and happiness. My heart is full. My purpose is staying connected to my heart. I surrender to this purpose.

– TRUST

I trust in God's heavenly plan for happiness. I am learning to trust others. I am learning to trust myself. I trust everything is always working out for me. I am worthy. I trust my intuition. I trust my boundaries. I am healing. I am vulnerable. My heart is open. I trust everything is working the way it's supposed to. I am authentic. I am a good friend. I trust myself. I am committed to myself. I am committed to my health. I am committed to taking care of my heart.

I trust everything will be okay. I trust my mentors. I trust that my journey is going well. I trust that I am on my way to living my dream life. I trust everything is falling into place. I am trusting that others have my best interest at heart. I am taking action on everything. I deserve abundance. I deserve to be cherished. I am feminine energy. I am radiant. I am confident. I am sincere. I trust my feelings. I am beautiful. I am pretty. I am attractive. I am comfortable with being me. My heart is full of love.

– ACCEPTANCE

I am committed to me. I am worthy of only high-value energy. I am a receiver of good energy. The Holy Spirit breathes in this high energy. I am here to take care of myself and to stay committed to me. I'm feeling good. I'm feeling aligned. Things are always working out for me. Money flows to me easily and effortlessly every single day. I am full of love, joy, and happiness that regenerates over and over and over again. All of these good sensations are what I attract and become. I attract everything I am creating. I make peace with my looks. My beauty is my energy. I am a magnet that attracts the abundance I desire. I'm committed to myself. I surrender to my purpose of staying connected to my heart. I surrender to allowing everything I desire. I am worth everything that comes my way. The Holy Spirit is my inspiration. My purpose is staying connected to the love in my heart. I deserve love. My value is not in my perfection.

– RECEIVE

Trusting is my only strength. My true value is my energy. I am very valuable. I am worthy of abundance just because of who I am. I am a receiver of good energy. I look to receive good energy. My true power is receiving everything I'm being given. I receive everything naturally with joy. I am a high-value woman. My energy comes from my loving heart. I am worthy of receiving good energy. I am worthy because I am me. I love myself. I trust in God's heavenly plan for true happiness. None of my plans or my creations could compare. I am so grateful for this journey. My pain makes my soul stronger. I've always been alone, and I've never liked it. It hurts my heart. I'm the only one who can make me happy. Trusting is how I take care of my heart. I am grateful.

What am I here to learn? I am the only who can make myself feel safe and secure. The love, joy, happiness, and abundance I deserve is already in my heart. I am a magnet.

WEEK 13

– EMPOWERMENT

What am I here to learn? I am in love with happiness. I make myself happy. What is God's plan for me? I am not here to endure pain. Pain is my strength. I was brought into this world for love. I am love. I can trust God's heavenly plan. Everything is always working out for me. I can enjoy the journey. I take care of my heart. I am finding my inner voice. Experiencing these thoughts are making me stronger.

Being vulnerable is my strength. My heart is my confidence. Staying connected to my physical self makes me more magnetic. My energy is my strength. My confidence comes from my heart. The Holy Spirit fills me with love, joy, and abundance. I am connected to myself. I am here to protect my heart. My true power is trusting and knowing. I will have the words. Everything will work out better than I can ever plan. My truth is my feminine energy. I am soft, sacred feminine energy. I attract positive energy. I deserve abundance and positive energy.

– FEEL

What am I feeling? What am I running away from?

What am I here to learn? My feelings are my power. My authenticity is my core power. I am growing from this pain. My feelings are my guide. My feelings are my intuition. My heart is open. My purpose is staying connected to my pain. That is truth. Staying connected to the hurt and pain helps me connect to my heart. I am my authentic feelings. My feelings are my strength—and not feelings of shame. I am magnetic energy. I radiate love, joy, and happiness from my heart. I'm ready to face my fears. My feeling force is my power. I honor my inner goddess. I am sacred, soft energy. I am a goddess. I am powerful and valuable. I am beautiful and radiant. I am the only one of me. I receive the energy of the Holy Spirit in my heart. My skin glows and glistens. I am safe. As a goddess, I know expressing my emotions is what heals me. I embrace me. I embrace my vulnerability. I am connected to fullness.

What am I here to learn? I want love, joy, and happiness. I deserve love, joy and happiness. I trust in God's heavenly plan for happiness. I honor myself and protect my heart by facing my fears.

– TRUST

I am valuable. I am feminine energy. My power is my deeper soul. I trust myself. I show up for me. I show up for my heart. Everything is always working out for me. There must be value in this. I am stronger. My vulnerability is my strength. My heart is my strength. I surrender to my purpose and staying connected to my heart. My truth is love, joy, and abundance. I trust in God's heavenly plan. I am trustworthy. I have found myself. I am grateful for my soft, sacred feminine energy. I honor my feminine center. I honor myself. My transparency is my strength. Everything is working out the way it's supposed to. I trust in God's plan. I'm prepared. I love myself. I give and receive love freely. My value is not in my perfection.

– ACCEPTANCE

What am I allowing? What am I forcing? Pushing forward and shoving does not serve me. Everything I desire is waiting for me. The Holy Spirit breathes inspiration into me. I soften and surrender to God's plan. It's my job to trust. I know that God has more to offer than I can imagine. I am attracting abundance and everything I desire. Everything I desire will come to me. This is an opportunity for me to grow. I am full. I regenerate and am resourcing energy over and over with love, joy, and happiness. I am a goddess. My energy is soft and sacred. I trust myself. I am the source of everything I want. I am what I think. My online business is my focus.

What am I here to learn? I am worthy of everything that comes my way. I deserve abundance flowing to me easily and effortlessly every single day. My feminine energy allows this abundance. I breath in effortlessly. Health, wealth, and happiness flows to me effortlessly.

– RECEIVE

I am here for myself. My value is my energy. I show up for me. I am worthy of receiving good energy. My gift to others is my energy. My energy is love. I am centered in my energy. I am a receiver of good energy.

The Holy Spirit regenerates through me with every single breath. I am worthy because of my energy. I am a good receiver. I am present in every moment. I am fully enjoying every experience. I am a receiver of good energy. Everything is working out for me. My core power comes from within me. I am a loving heart. I value myself. I am an elevated high-value woman. I am soft, sacred feminine energy. I am worthy of receiving amazing things. Knowing my value helps me receive all the good things I desire. I am worthy of everything I want because I am me. Others want to give to me—and I am open to receiving abundance. I am ready to receive. My power lies in my ability to receive. I am magnetic energy that attracts everything I desire. I naturally radiate soft, sacred feminine energy with every breath. My beauty is on the inside. My beauty radiates on the outside and others feel it. My heart is open.

WEEK 14

– EMPOWERMENT

What am I? I am expanding more of who I am. I am experiencing pain. My power comes from my heart. I am here to connect to my pain. My pain is my strength. I am attracting everything I need in my life. My strength comes from staying grounded in my body. I am grounded in myself. Everything I want is attracted to me. Trusting is my strength. My truth comes from my heart. I can hurt. It's okay to hurt.

What am I here to learn? God has a heavenly plan that I'll never understand. My strength comes from allowing what God has planned—and not from me creating it. It's time for me to let go of control. I am here to take care of myself. My life brings me joy. Protecting my heart is my passion. I am a goddess. I deserve respect. I am an elevated woman. I am worthy of receiving only positive energy. I am soft, sacred feminine energy. I receive abundance. I am worthy of receiving abundance. The Holy Spirit pours abundant energy on me. I am a receiver of love, joy, and abundance. I am born to thrive.

– FEEL

I am strong. My strength is my energy. Abundance is flowing easily and effortlessly to me every single day. My purpose is staying connected to my heart. My pain is my strength. My pain makes me stronger every day. My feelings are my guide.

What am I here to learn? My feelings are my guide. I trust in God's heavenly plan. I am authentic. I am open. I am a receiver. I am unique. I am beautiful. My awareness comes from my feelings. I love myself. I give myself permission to give love and receive love freely. I radiate love, joy, and happiness. The Holy Spirit radiates through me. The Holy Spirit regenerates this energy over and over. I am worthy of holding and receiving this abundant energy. I honor myself. I honor my feelings. I honor my heart. I honor my soft, sacred feminine energy. I love myself. I make myself feel safe and secure. Everything flows to me easily and effortlessly. I am grateful for this journey. I truly am feminine energy, and feel stronger and more confident than ever before. I love me. I'm good enough. I have harmony within myself. I am not perfect. I don't need to be perfect. I am me. I love myself. I take care of myself. Everything is perfect the way it is. I am whole. I am perfect as I am. I am completely at peace. I am completely present. I am centered in my own essence. I am positive energy. I am enough. I am fullness. All is well. I dwell in this moment as the Holy Spirit fills me up. The Holy Spirit makes everything perfect. Nothing exists but the here and now. Everything comes to me effortlessly. I am at peace. Love is the energy that fuels me—not fear.

– TRUST

I am becoming a deeper soul. I am soft, sacred energy. I am what I tell myself. My heart is open. I came into the world for love. My purpose is staying connected to my heart. My vulnerability is my strength. I am love. I am loving. I am loved. I take care of me. I create my own happiness. I make myself feel safe and secure. I don't have to suffer to find happiness. Happiness comes from within me. My pain makes me stronger. Everything is always working out for me. There must be value in this. I trust in God's heavenly plan. My pain is my strength. I trust myself. I am trustworthy. I am here for me. My confidence comes from my heart. My heart is magnetic energy. I am committed to myself. I am worthy of everything I desire. I am a gift. I cherish myself. The Holy Spirit radiates love, joy, and happiness through me. I am worthy of abundance. I am not perfect. I am sacred energy. I deserve abundance. Abundance flows through me easily and effortlessly every single day. I am good enough. I am who I am.

— ACCEPTANCE

What am I here to learn? Any low and negative feelings filling my head do not serve me, and they keep my vibration low. I only attract good energy. I trust in God's heavenly plan. I know this will all work out. It will work out better than I can ever imagine. Things are always working for me. What is the next logical step? Everything is falling together the way it's supposed to. Everything is okay. This is an opportunity to grow. I'm being taught something here. My pain is strengthening my soul. The Holy Spirit is regenerating the energy of love, joy, and abundance in my soul.

I radiate fullness. I am full of soft, sacred feminine energy. I make peace with where I am. I am here every morning for me. I am the source of everything I want. I am what I think, and my life is a result of my positive mind-set. I can't force anything. I am here for me. I am the creator of everything I desire. My strength is trusting. I am worthy of everything that comes my way. I am worthy of everything I desire.

— RECEIVE

My heart needs my love. The Holy Spirit lives in me. The Holy Spirit regenerates more of who I am over and over. The Holy Spirit fills me with joy, love, and abundance. I give myself love. I listen to my heart. I am good enough. I am worthy of love, joy, and abundances. I have learned how to feel safe and secure again. Everything is always working out. I am perfect. I am God's child. I am good enough. I am not in control. God has an amazing plan for me. It's a plan I can't even imagine. I am stuck where I am, but I can look for love, joy, and abundance. I can learn from others every day.

I'm scared and my heart is full of love. I deserve love. I am worthy. I am a receiver of good energy. I deserve to receive only good energy. I am a high-value woman. My value is my loving heart. My feminine energy is soft and sacred. Everything I desire I deserve because I am worthy. I'm ready to receive from myself. I deserve deep love. I deserve deep happiness. I deserve deep joy. I deserve deep abundance. I radiate this beautiful soft, sacred energy.

WEEK 15

– EMPOWERMENT

I am grateful for this journey. My power is centered in my energy. Vulnerability is my strength. I trust in God's heavenly plan. Everything is always working out for me. I am attracting abundant energy. I am attracting everything I need in life. I am magnetic. I am pulling the whole world towards me. I am grounded in myself. I am regenerating positive energy. I am soft, sacred feminine energy. My confidence comes from my body and my feelings. My heart is open.

Empowered energy flows through me in every moment and every day. Everything I desire naturally comes to me. My pain gives me strength. My vulnerability makes me stronger. Everything is okay. The Holy Spirit breathes deep love, deep joy, and deep abundance in me. God's plan is better than I can ever imagine. Trusting is my strength. My energy is my beauty. My loving presence is my greatest gift. I am the energy I desire. My purpose is my loving heart.

– FEEL

Trusting is my strength. I want to trust. What am I avoiding? I don't need to come up with the solution. My heart is open. I am trustworthy. I journal and mediate every day for me. My emotions make me who I am. I trust in God's heavenly plan. Taking care of my heart is most important. I am an elevated woman. I deserve honor and respect. My confidence comes from my heart. I surrender to my purpose. My heart and feelings are magnetic. Trusting my magnetic energy is my strength.

What am I feeling? Everything will be okay. I make mistakes, and then I fix them. I am a leader. I am an influencer. Everything I feel makes me stronger. I learn something new and become stronger. My power as a woman comes from my energy. How do I step up and keep myself grounded? I am grateful for my heart. My courage is building. I trust myself. I show up for me. I need closure on so many things. The only closure that will come is with one step at a time. What I am feeling is okay. I trust in God's plan for happiness. I am grateful for this journey.

– TRUST

All I have is me. I'm the only person I can count on. I'm shy. How is being shy serving me? I must be getting something out of it. My heart hurts. Vulnerability is my strength. Imperfection is my strength. I'm tired of fear. I'm tired of being afraid. My strength comes from my open heart. I trust in God's heavenly plan for happiness. I trust everything is always working out for me. Trusting is my strength. My true feminine power is trusting that things are always working out for me. My intuition tells me to trust. Where am I not trusting myself? I take care of myself. I love myself. I am sacred energy.

– ACCEPTANCE

I am soft, sacred feminine energy. I am committed to taking care of myself and my energy. Everything is working out for me. I am a receiver of good energy. My heart is full of love. My heart is open. Trusting is my strength. I am smart. I am prepared. I feel good. I am attracting everything I want. I am trusting God's heavenly plan. Everything is okay. I am full of amazing positive regenerating energy. I meditate with love, joy, and abundance. I am worthy of everything I desire. I am at peace with where I am. I am trustworthy. My life is full of abundance. I am what I think. I am love. Positive things are happening to me. The Holy Spirit is flowing energy to me. My energy comes from inside of me. I am everything I desire. I am worthy of everything that comes my way. I am love. Love brings happiness. I accept where I am by simply being me and being grateful for this journey. I was brought in this world to love and show others love. My energy is love, joy, and abundance.

– RECEIVE

My worthiness lies in my energy. My energy is my gift to others. My feminine energy is a magnetic pull. I am very valuable, and it comes from my energy. Receiving energy is my gift to others. Trusting is my gift. My core power comes from within. My soul is beautiful. I am a beautiful person. I am a high-value woman. I am valuable. My purpose is staying connected to my heart. I deserve love, happiness, and abundance. I am worthy of success in my business. I am ready to manifest everything I desire. Abundance flows to me easily and effortlessly every single day. The Holy Spirit fills me with joy. I am here to receive all this joy. Joy and love live in my heart. I radiate deep love, deep happiness, and deep abundance. I feel the fullness of my body with my breath. I am beautiful. I am soft, sacred feminine energy. I value every bit of energy inside of me. I acknowledge who I really am.

WEEK 16

– EMPOWERMENT

I am learning. I am a forgiven child of God. My pain is my strength. I own my mistakes. I forgive myself. Trusting is my strength. My wisdom comes from my feelings and my body. My mind doesn't really know how to solve problems. Feeling this pain and experiencing my pain is my strength. Focusing on the pain in my body is my strength.

I am here to learn. Trusting is my strength. All I have is me. I forgive myself. Staying inside of my body is my strength. Staying inside of my body is my feminine energy. Feeling inside of me is how I will resolve my pain. I am worthy of abundance. I am worthy of forgiveness. The Holy Spirit breathes deep love, deep happiness, and deep abundance inside of me. My mind can't solve this. I need to feel the pain.

– FEEL

I don't need validation from anyone else. I am attracting everything I want in my life. My heart is full of love, joy, and happiness. That is what I am attracting. My purpose is staying connected to my heart. I face my pain. My pain makes me grow. My pain makes me deeper. My feelings are my best friends. Looking for solutions doesn't give me peace. Releasing judgment keeps me out of my head, which gives me more confidence. My power as a woman is my energy. I am open and vulnerable. I am authentic. I am valuable soft, sacred feminine energy. I am committed to me. I am committed to my feelings. I love myself. I give myself permission to give love and receive love freely.

– TRUST

I am energy. I am magnetic. My power is my heart.

What am I here to learn? I am love. I come from love. My vibration is love. Everything I desire is inside me. My beauty is inside of me. I trust God's heavenly plan. All of my fears come from not knowing. Trusting God is my strength. My wounds are the source of my beauty.

What am I here to learn? What is my pain? What are my fears. I embrace my pain. I embrace my loneliness. I love myself. I protect my heart. I am soft, sacred feminine energy. My heart is open. Being neutral is my goal. My ego has to step away by becoming neutral. I am softness. My energy is my strength. I attract only warm, positive energy. My feminine energy is my power. I am a goddess. I am discovering my elevated goddess energy.

What am I here to learn? My power comes from staying out of my head. My power comes from trusting. My power comes from staying neutral. The Holy Spirit breathes love, joy, and abundance in me. My energy vibrates love. I honor my heart.

– ACCEPTANCE

What am I here to learn? I deserve abundance. I trust in God's heavenly plan for happiness. I feel good. The Holy Spirit breathes more and more love inside of me. I surrender to my weakness. I can trust myself and my inner wisdom. Everything is working out the way it's supposed to. Everything is okay. I am here to learn. I am not empty. I am a full, fluid, and dynamic body that's regenerating over and over again. My law of attraction is fullness. I am peace. I am what I think. My heart is full of love. I am ready to receive love from the Holy Spirit. I'm not in control. I am worthy of everything that comes my way. I am worthy of what I want. I am sacred energy. My heart is my strength. I took this journey to find my confidence. My confidence comes from my loving heart. Speaking up and protecting my heart means I am taking care of myself. I love myself deeply.

What am I here to learn? I am becoming a better person. I trust that God has a bigger and better plan for me. My job is to take care of me. Everything is going to work out for me. I am ready to receive abundance. I am amazing energy.

– RECEIVE

Abundance flows to me easily and effortlessly every single day. I trust in God's heavenly plan for happiness. My confidence comes from my feminine energy. The Holy Spirit fills my heart with love, joy, and abundance. My feminine energy is my confidence. I surrender to my purpose. My purpose is staying connected to my heart. My heart is open. I am soft, sacred feminine energy. I am worthy of receiving abundance. Everything is always working out for me. I am magnetic energy. I am beautiful and magnetic. I am very valuable, and it comes from my energy. I am who I am. I embrace who I am. I am a receiver of good energy. My strength is fully experiencing what I am receiving. My gift is receiving. I believe in my value. I am a loving soul. My vulnerability and my pain are my strength. My worth comes from how I feel inside. I am valuable. I am worthy of everything I desire. I am ready to receive abundance. I am ready to receive life. I am ready to face my fears and not worry how things will turn out. I am here to learn and grow. I am grateful for this journey. I radiate deep love. I am love.

WEEK 17

– EMPOWERMENT

What am I here to learn? I am so grateful for this journey. I trust in God's plan for heavenly happiness. My confidence comes from my heart. I trust myself. I am here for myself. My magnetic energy pulls everything I need in my life. Staying connected in my heart and my soft, sacred energy is magnetic.

My energy is my confidence. Getting inside of every moment is my strength. Slowing down the tempo helps me experience every moment while it's happening. Feeling every moment all the time pulls everything to me. Everything I desire naturally comes to me. I am worthy of everything I desire. Everything I desire naturally comes to me. Everything is always working out for me. My heart is open. My pain and vulnerability are my strength. I am open to receiving everything I desire. Everything is always working out for me. My heart is open. I am open to receiving deep love, deep joy, and deep abundance. The Holy Spirit regenerates this energy into me over and over again.

I attract only positive energy. My loving presence is my gift to others. I know there's a plan, but it's not mine. I'm neutral. It's not mine for the taking. Staying neutral is the only thing I can control. My heart hurts. Only I can make me feel safe and secure. Trusting is my feminine energy. I trust God's plan. God's plan is always better than what I can create. I want to run away. My pain is my strength. My vulnerability is my strength. God has a plan for me—and it's not for me to screw up.

WEEK 18

– EMPOWERMENT

Everything I desire is being attracted to me. I surrender to my purpose of staying connected to my heart. I deserve abundance. The Holy Spirit regenerates deep love and deep abundance inside of me. I'm not afraid. My confidence comes from my heart. I trust in God's heavenly plan for happiness. My strength is that I have no plan. Love is my essence. Staying in the moment keeps me in my feminine energy. My loving presence is my gift to others. My heart is open.

I am committed to myself. I am excited to be on this journey. Abundance flows abundantly in my life. I am beautiful. I am attractive. I don't need anyone's love to make me feel secure. I am worthwhile. I love me. I'm the only person I can truly count on. I honor myself and am proud of who I am. I am worthy of loving myself. I am healing. I am getting stronger every day. This is my truth. I am experiencing life more fully. I am anchored to the earth. I am radiant. I am healthy. My skin is healthy. My skin glows.

What am I here to learn? I am on this journey to find me and to find my confidence. My confidence comes from my energy which I have avoided all my life. I never knew my purpose. My purpose is to stay connected to my heart.

– FEEL

My feelings are valuable. I deserve respect. I respect myself. I am trustworthy. I am disappointed in myself that I couldn't find the courage to speak up. I am disappointed in myself for not being honest—and for not showing my vulnerability. My feelings are important. My pain is important. My emotions are my strength. I will be okay. I make mistakes. I am a forgiven child of God. God has a plan. I am here to live God's plan. My feminine energy is my core power. I am experiencing a lot of pain right now. I am becoming more of me every day. My heart is open. My purpose is staying connected to my heart. Staying in my head doesn't serve me. I am healing. I am becoming a high-elevated woman with higher potential of abundance. I am grateful. I honor myself. I honor my heart. My true power as a woman are my feelings. My inner strength is my beauty. I deserve positive energy. Everything will be okay. I trust in God's heavenly plan for true happiness.

– TRUST

I am here because I trust myself. I can handle any situation that comes my way. I am learning through every experience. My true value and worth comes from my heart. What am I here to learn next? This doesn't feel right to me. I'm feeling hurt and disappointment. Everything is always working out for me. I trust in God's heavenly plan. I'm confused. Trusting is my strength. Trusting is my vulnerability. My heart is warm and loving. I surrender to my purpose of staying connected to my heart. I forgive myself. I forgive myself for not trusting. Where do I not trust myself? My heart is hurting. I am here for me. I am committed to taking care of my heart. I trust in God's heavenly plan for happiness. My confidence comes from my heart. I am love. I am full of love. I'm not feeling loved. It hurts. This feeling is making me stronger.

The Holy Spirit regenerates and fills me with deep love, deep happiness, and deep abundance. My gentleness and vulnerability are my shield. I am becoming more of me. My power is feeling my pain. I cherish myself. My true power as a woman is my heart. I am soft, sacred feminine energy. I am secure in myself. I am a goddess of fullness. I forgive myself. I surrender to God's plan. I have no plan. I have no expectation. I am not in control. I am neutral. My frequency is neutral. I choose trust. I don't choose fear. I am responsible for me, and I trust in God's heavenly plan. I am here to exist for the Holy Spirit to fill my heart with love. I am committed to being neutral.

– ACCEPTANCE

What am I here to learn? Allowing attracts anything I want. I have no plan. My feminine energy is my power place. My confidence comes from my heart. The Holy Spirit fills me with love. Trusting is my strength. Everything is working out the way it's supposed to. Everything is okay. This is something I'm being taught. I am a full energy. I regenerate love, joy, and abundance. I am dynamic. I am full of good sensations. I am making peace with where I am. I am what I think. I attract only positive energy. I am the creator of everything I desire. My purpose in life is staying connected to my heart. My attraction is my energy. I am worthy of everything that comes my way. I am worthy of love, joy, and abundance. I am soft, sacred feminine energy. I am love.

– RECEIVE

I allow only good energy. I am here to receive. I don't understand, but it's not my plan. I trust in God's heavenly plan. My worthiness lies in my energy. My feminine energy is my gift. Staying connected to my heart is my power. This is how I am valuable. The Holy Spirit breathes divine love, joy, and abundance in my heart. I am a receiver of this soft, sacred feminine energy. I am forgiven. I forgive myself. I am love. I give myself permission to give love and receive love freely. The universe breathes through me. I am the source of everything I desire. I am magnetic energy. I radiate deep love, deep joy, and deep abundance through my energy. I am beautiful divine energy.

WEEK 19

– EMPOWERMENT

What am I here to learn? My confidence comes from staying in my heart. I surrender to my purpose of staying connected to my heart. Resentment doesn't serve me. I am soft, sacred feminine energy. My gift to others is my loving presence. I am magnetic energy. Experiencing the moment allows me to be me. Staying connected to myself is my strength. I love me. I take care of me. Shutting off my brain is my strength.

My feminine energy is my confidence. I am soft, sacred feminine energy. My feminine energy is my power. Trusting is my strength. Staying connected to my heart is my purpose. Everything is always working out for me. I am love. I am loving. I am loved. I trust in God's heavenly plan for happiness. Everything I need comes from inside of me. I am grateful for this journey. I have been blessed. I am grateful to experience every moment. Finding myself is my strength. Happiness comes from my heart. I love myself. The Holy Spirit fills me up with deep love, deep happiness, and deep abundance. My greatest gift is my loving presence.

– FEEL

Who am I? What am I feeling? I want to run away. I'm afraid. I'm hurt. My feelings are my power.

What am I here to learn? I want to protect my heart. I am becoming stronger. My depth is my strength. I am open to my feelings. I trust God's heavenly plan. My energy is my power. I am becoming fuller of who I am. I want to attract only people who love me. I am not ashamed of my feelings. My purpose is staying connected to my heart. My emptiness is my pain. I am sacred energy. I am infinity. The Holy Spirit fills me up and makes me who I am. Feeling my pain helps me connect to my higher energy.

My feminine energy is my strength. I own my power. I trust the process. I trust that journaling is a process that brings out my confidence. Perfection is not my strength. Vulnerability is my strength. My feminine energy is magnetic. I am goddess energy. I am always discovering more of myself. I am being called to be courageous. I am chaos. I am wildness. I am strength. My confidence comes from my heart. My confidence comes from my softness. I choose my power over my fear. I feel my fear. I embrace my fear. I embrace my pain. I honor myself. I honor my feelings. I attract divine love.

– TRUST

My heart is heavy. I'm confused.

What am I here to learn? This journey is about me finding myself. This journey is about finding my confidence and my inner strength.

What am I here to learn? I know God has a plan. I don't have to have the plan. I know things will work out. Everything will be okay. Assuming I have only myself is not my truth. I am good enough. I am pretty enough. I am magnetic energy. Everything is always working out for me. My pain is my strength. I am here to learn. I am becoming a deeper soul. There must be value in this. I am here to trust myself. Everything will work out. I am a warm, loving soul. I surrender to myself and taking care of myself. I surrender to staying connected to my heart. My loving heart is my confidence. My vulnerability is my strength. I love me. I am here for myself. I show up for myself. I am committed to me. Only I can give myself the love I deserve. Everything I need to understand is inside of me. My loving presence and my loving heart are my true strength. My gentleness and awareness are my vulnerability. I have to take care of me.

– ACCEPTANCE

Shutting off my brain is my strength. I am a receiver of good energy. Trusting is my strength. I trust in God's heavenly plan. My feminine energy is trusting and allowing. Everything is okay. Everything is working out. I am regenerating fullness and I'm filled with all the good sensations. I am worthy of love, joy, and abundance. I am becoming the person I've always wanted to be. I am the source of everything I've always wanted to be. My confidence comes from my heart. My happiness and security come from inside me. I am the creator of everything I desire. I trust myself. I honor myself. I am worthy of everything that comes my way. The Holy Spirit fills me up and inspires me. I am filled with positive and soft, sacred feminine energy. I am worthy of everything I want. My loving presence brings everything my way. I am manifesting everything I want towards me. Everything flows abundantly to me. I am worthy of this energy. Abundance flows easily and effortlessly to me every single day. My soft, sacred feminine energy is my strength.

– RECEIVE

What am I here to learn? My heart is open. I am a receiver of good energy. I am worthy of happiness and abundance. I surrender to my vulnerability. My gift to others is my loving presence. My courage comes from my deeper feelings. I am worthy of everything I desire. I surrender to my purpose of staying connected to my heart. I receive good energy just because of who I am. I am ready to receive. I don't know the plan. Everything is always working out for me. I am valuable. I want to receive. I understand my value. I am anchored in my truth. I am a beautiful person. I am worthy of receiving positive energy. I am valuable and I'm worthy of everything I desire. I deserve abundance and I am worthy of it because that's my desire. I am afraid of what is being given to me. I'm afraid to be a receiver. I trust in God's heavenly plan for happiness. My magnetic energy attracts everything I desire. I am full. I naturally radiate abundance and happiness. The Holy Spirit fills me up over and over again. I radiate this beauty. My true power is my energy. But I'm afraid. I want to run. Running won't serve me. Love is my truth.

WEEK 20

– EMPOWERMENT

What am I here to learn? I am grateful for this journey. I am grateful for love. My heart is open. My confidence comes from my purpose. I surrender to my purpose of staying connected to my heart. I trust in God's plan for happiness. I don't need to know any other plan. I can't create a better plan.

Trusting is my strength. My pain makes me stronger. Staying connected to my heart is my strength. I can handle anything that comes my way. Everything is always working out for me. Staying connected to my body attracts everything I desire. I am pulling the whole world to me by staying connected to my body. The Holy Spirit fills me with my true power. The Holy Spirit fills me with love. Experiencing every moment helps me stay connected to my body which magnetizes everyone to me.

I am worthy of attracting abundance. Everything I desire is naturally being attracted to me. My feminine energy is my strength. I am soft, sacred feminine energy that regenerates over and over. My greatest gift is my presence.

What am I here to learn? I want to feel my feelings. My feelings are mine to feel. I can't make anyone else feel my feelings. I feel pain and hurt. My power is taking on my deeper feelings. I'm afraid. My feelings are my guide. My heart is open. I surrender to my purpose of staying connected to my heart. Every experience makes me fuller. My feminine energy is dynamic. I am authentic. I attract only people who are authentic and are positive. It's important to work with my emotions. Feeling my emotion makes my soul stronger. I am not ashamed of my emotions. My heart is full of love. I connect only with heart-to-heart connections. My inner strength is part of my beauty. I honor my inner strength. I honor my inner child. Staying small does not serve me. Moving out of my comfort zone is my strength.

Fear is an emotion I'm feeling. Living in fear doesn't serve me. Facing my fear helps me grow. Facing my fear serves me. Being afraid doesn't serve me. I choose trust over fear. I commit to trust. I trust in God's heavenly plan for happiness. How will I be receiving abundance? I deserve abundance. I live at an elevated frequency. My heart is open. I'm here to learn. I am gentleness. I am soft, sacred feminine energy. My energy comes from the Holy Spirit which continues to give and flow through me. This energy is my vibration and frequency. I am filled up by this energy. I am abundance. I am worthy of this frequency. I am worthy of abundance.

– FEEL

What am I here to learn? I want to feel my feelings. My feelings are mine to feel. I can't make anyone else feel my feelings. I feel pain and hurt. My power is taking on my deeper feelings. I'm afraid. My feelings are my guide. My heart is open. I surrender to my purpose of staying connected to my heart. Every experience makes me fuller. My feminine energy is dynamic. I am authentic. I attract only people who are authentic and are positive. It's important to work with my emotions. Feeling my emotion makes my soul stronger. I am not ashamed of my emotions. My heart is full of love. I connect only with heart-to-heart connections. My inner strength is part of my beauty. I honor my inner strength. I honor my inner child. Staying small does not serve me. Moving out of my comfort zone is my strength.

Fear is an emotion I'm feeling. Living in fear doesn't serve me. Facing my fear helps me grow. Facing my fear serves me. Being afraid doesn't serve me. I choose trust over fear. I commit to trust. I trust in God's heavenly plan for happiness. How will I be receiving abundance? I deserve abundance. I live at an elevated frequency. My heart is open. I'm here to learn. I am gentleness. I am soft, sacred feminine energy.

My energy comes from the Holy Spirit which continues to give and flow through me. This energy is my vibration and frequency. I am filled by this energy. I am abundance. I am worthy of this frequency. I am worthy of abundance.

– TRUST

I'm scared. Trusting is my strength.

What am I here to learn? Self-trust is my strength. Everything is always working out for me. I have to trust myself. My pain is my power. Feeling my vulnerability serves me. My loving presence is my gift to others. What is my truth? I surrender to my purpose of staying connected to my heart. I am committed to me. I am showing up for myself. Things aren't working out perfectly, and my brain is on overload, but I will be okay. I want to solve this, and I don't know how, yet I will be okay. My strength comes from trusting and allowing, not creating. God has a plan, and those plans are better than anything I can create. Playing safe doesn't serve me. I can only trust that everything will work out for me.

– ACCEPTANCE

I am love. I am sacred energy. I am worthy of abundance. I trust in God's heavenly plan. I surrender to my purpose of staying connected to my heart. Trusting is my strength. My heart is open. Things are always working out for me. Everything is okay. I am full-fluid dynamic energy regenerating love, joy, and abundance over and over again. I am attracting the thoughts that are inside of me. I am making peace with where I am. I am the source of everything I want. I am what I think. I am magical. I am magnetic energy. My true power as a woman is my soft, sacred feminine energy. I am worthy of abundance. Abundance flows to me easily and effortlessly every day. With every breath, the Holy Spirit fills me with inspiration. Everything is attracted to me because I am connected to the deep love in my heart. The flow of love pours inside of me. I am grateful for this journey. Trusting is my strength. Allowing is my gift.

– RECEIVE

What am I here to learn? I am a receiver of good energy. My worthiness lies in my energy. I am beautiful valuable energy. The Holy Spirit fills my heart with love. I am worthy of everything I desire because of who I am. I trust in God's heavenly plan for happiness. I deserve abundance. I am worthy of receiving amazing things.

What am I here to learn? What am I here to receive? My inspiration comes from receiving. My power lies in the ability to receive. My gift to the world is my loving presence. I naturally radiate my loving energy. I am sacred soft feminine energy. Everything I desire is inside me. I radiate deep love, deep happiness, and deep abundance. The Holy Spirit radiates this energy inside of me over and over again.

WEEK 21

– EMPOWERMENT

I honor myself. I deserve honor. What is my truth? I am grateful for this journey. I am grateful for finding myself. I love myself. I forgive myself. I have compassion for myself. I am sacred, soft feminine energy. I surrender to my purpose of staying connected to my heart.

Honoring myself elevates me. I deserve honor. I am worthy of abundance. I trust in God's plan for heavenly happiness. God has a plan for me on earth that *I don't understand*, but I don't need to. I take care of myself. I love myself. I found myself. I deserve abundance. I am the only one who can take care of me. I want to be taken care of. I want to receive.

My confidence comes from my body and my feelings. I only attract good energy. I am here for myself. I am magnetic energy. I am connected to myself. I am attracting everything I need in my life. Staying grounded in myself gives me power. Trusting gives me strength. I acknowledge my empowered life comes from my energy within me. I experience everything from my true feminine center.

I can't be manipulated. I won't be manipulated. I deserve elevated positive energy. Humility serves me. The Holy Spirit breathes love, joy, and abundance in me. *I don't understand. I don't need to understand.* I am centered in my feminine energy. I don't need to have a plan. I am a joyful receiver. *I don't like being manipulated. I don't understand. I don't need to understand.* I trust in God's heavenly plan. *I don't understand.* My loving presence is my gift. My fear and my pain give me strength. I want to hide because I am afraid to face my pain.

What am I here to learn? Trusting is my strength. Humility is so hard. I believe in myself. I need to find happiness in my heart. Only I can give myself happiness.

– FEEL

I'm afraid. My feelings are my power. I am connected to my energy. I am becoming deeper and stronger in my own self. My feelings are my best friends. I trust in God's heavenly plan. I am open to God's plan. My power as a woman lies in my energy. I am dynamic. I am authentic. I am who I am. I connect to my heart. I am going to be okay. My feelings are my power place. I need to forgive myself. I am attracting everything I desire. I feel shame. I feel guilt. These feelings are my strength. This pain is another experience of life. I am a good person. I am worthy of abundance. I am a forgiven child of God. I love myself. I take care of my feelings. My heart is love. My life is full. I am love. I am soft, sacred energy. My strength comes from trusting. I am a blessing. I am grateful for this journey. I am here to learn. I love my inner child.

– TRUST

I am committed to taking care of me. I am committed to trusting myself. I am vulnerable. I am healing. I can trust myself. I am connected to my true value. I am a deeper soul. I listen to my heart. I trust everything is always working for me. All of the answers are inside of me. My suffering is my strength. I am on a journey of abundance and finding myself. I am embracing this journey. This journey is amazing and is making me happy. I deserve happiness. I deserve abundance. I trust God's heavenly plan for happiness. The Holy Spirit fills me up with love.

– ACCEPTANCE

What am I here to learn? My faith is a core value. How can I become better? I am so grateful for finding myself. I am here to protect my "me." I surrender to my purpose of staying connected to my heart.

What am I here to learn? My goal is to surrender. Trusting is my strength. I am learning how to embrace surrendering. My heart is open. My heart is full of love. The Holy Spirit fills my heart with love, joy, and abundance. I regenerate this loving, soft, sacred energy with every breath. I trust God's heavenly plan for happiness. I can only trust God's plan. Any plans I create cannot compare. Trusting is my strength. Trusting is my courage. My vulnerability is my courage. Everything is always working out for me. I am magnetic energy. Abundance flows to me. I don't know how things will work out, but I trust everything is always working out for me. I feel better when I'm allowing. I don't have to chase or pull. Abundance is attracted to me.

Everything is working out the way it's supposed to. Everything is okay. This is another opportunity for me to learn another new lesson. I am full, feminine energy. I am dynamic and gorgeous feminine energy. I meditate with love, joy, and happiness. I attract only the positive energy I create inside of me. I am a forgiven, loving child of God. I forgive myself. Living in shame and fear do not serve me. I am at peace with where I am. I am neutral. I take care of me.

My greatest power is learning from my pain. Allowing positive energy is what serves me. I am source. I am worth everything I desire. I am worthy of abundance. Everything will be okay. I am here to learn. I am abundance. Abundance is the presence of energy. My life is full of good energy. I am love. I am soft, sacred feminine energy. I deserve abundance. I allow only good energy to flow to me. My heart knows truth. My confidence comes from knowing myself. My confidence is my beauty. I am grateful for this journey.

− RECEIVE

I deserve happiness. I deserve abundance. My worthiness is my energy. I am beautiful. My energy is valuable. My heart is open. My energy is alive. I am worthy. I am feminine energy. I trust in God's heavenly plan. I experience everything through the Holy Spirit. I am feminine energy. I am valuable. I am comfortable receiving from others. I am worthy of amazing things. I am worthy because I am me. I am worthy of living every moment in my life. I am fun-loving. I am attractive. I manifest everything I desire in my life. I am the source of everything I desire. I am able to receive abundance. I allow abundance. Fun and radiance are attracted to me. My power is also in my ability to receive. I am a receiver. Abundance flows through me like fluid. Abundance flows in and out of me. I radiate abundance to others. I am happiness. I deserve happiness. I am magnetic. I attract abundance. I attract prosperity. I have access to all the energy I'll ever need. I am full and I continue to receive more and more. I deserve more.

WEEK 22

− EMPOWERMENT

My feminine energy is my strength. Trusting is my confidence. My power lies in experiencing every moment. I am an elevated woman. I am soft, sacred feminine energy. I trust myself. My body and my heart are magnetic energy. Staying connected to my physical body attracts everything I want into my life. I am pulling the whole world towards me. Staying grounded in my body gives me strength. Tending to my energy is what keeps me aligned.

My empowered life comes from inside of me. Abundance flows to me easily and effortlessly every single day. The Holy Spirit fills me with deep love, deep happiness, and deep abundance which regenerates in me over and over again. I trust in God's heavenly plan for happiness. I trust in God's plan. *I don't understand, and I don't need to understand.* Trusting is my strength. I hold Jesus' hand. My loving presence is my gift to others and to the world.

– FEEL

What am I feeling?

What am I here to learn? I'm feeling emptiness. My pain is my strength. I am becoming deeper as I feel this emptiness. I'm feeling empty because I can't control my life. My strength comes from trusting. I am open to learning from this emptiness. My heart is open. My heart is open to learning. This emptiness makes me sad. It's my choice to feel this way. My heart is feeling hurt and pain. It's okay to feel this way. I only have control over how I feel. I am a forgiven child of God. I'm worried. Worry doesn't serve me. What am I trying to control? When I worry, I don't trust God's plan. God's plan is better than any plan I can ever make. I trust in God's heavenly plan for happiness, which gives me peace. I am magnetic energy. I attract everything I desire. I am a feminine goddess. I attract deep love, deep happiness, and deep abundance. There is no plan I can make. My only plan is to keep trusting God. I trust my pain. My inner strength and inner wisdom are my confidence. My confidence is my beauty. Any shame I feel doesn't serve me. I let that go. I ask for forgiveness. I am a forgiven child of God.

– TRUST

I trust myself. I am trustworthy. I am committed to myself. I am committed to attracting abundance. I am worthy. I am receiving abundance. My value is in my self-worth. I am creating my own destiny. I trust everything is always working out for me. I love myself. My confidence comes from my heart. I trust everything is working out. I am trusting. The signs are reminders to take care of myself, and to breath. I focus on my every breath. The signs are my top priority that God wants me to remember my purpose to always feel from my heart. No one can make me happy but me. I can choose happiness. It hurts to know I'm the one who has to make me happy. It hurts so bad to know this. It makes me cry. I will be okay. I trust myself. I trust in God's plan. God has a heavenly plan. I look forward to God's heavenly joy and peace.

– ACCEPTANCE

I am sacred energy. I am soft, sacred feminine energy. I am grateful for this journey. Trusting is my strength. I trust in God's heavenly plan for happiness. My heart is full. The Holy Spirit regenerates deep love, deep happiness, and deep abundance inside of me. Everything is always working out for me. Trusting is my confidence. I am attracting everything I want in life. I'm afraid again. Everything is okay, and this is an opportunity for me to grow. I am a full-fluid dynamic energy. Fear is overcoming me. Abundance flows to me easily and effortlessly every day. My confidence comes from my heart. Everything I want is attracted to me. I am magnetic energy. Everything I want is attracted towards me. I am worth everything that comes my way. I am worthy. I am soft feminine energy. I can't hold myself back. Trusting is my strength. My vulnerability is my strength. I am love. I protect my heart. My confidence comes from allowing.

– RECEIVE

I am worthy. I am strong. I am soft, sacred feminine energy. I am growing every day. My pain is my strength. My masculine energy is my discipline. I am reaching for the stars and I am scared out of my mind. I trust in God's plan for happiness. There will be true happiness in heaven. I am grateful for this journey. Comparing myself doesn't serve me. I need to focus on my strengths. Showing up for myself is my strength. I am sacred energy. I am a receiver of good energy. My worthiness is my energy. My gift to others is my loving presence. Abundance flows to me easily and effortlessly every single day. I am a receiver of good energy because of who I am. I am worthy. I am worthy of abundance. My confidence comes from my loving heart. Surrendering to my purpose of staying connected to my heart is my confidence. Everything is always working out for me. I am worthy of everything I desire. The Holy Spirit gives to me. The Holy Spirit fills me with deep love, deep joy, and deep abundance.

WEEK 23

– EMPOWERMENT

What am I here to learn? What am I here to ask? My soft, sacred feminine energy is my confidence. Letting go calms my mind. My power and my energy are in my body. Centering myself in my body and in my heart gives me power. My heart attracts everything I desire. I can handle with grace anything that comes my way. I surrender to my purpose of staying connected to my heart. Staying connected to my heart pulls the whole world towards me.

Staying grounded gives me strength. I show up for me. My empowered life comes from inside of me. My feminine energy is magnetic. Experiencing every moment helps me feel my true power. Slowing down allows me to get inside of every moment. I have an abundance mindset. Everything I desire naturally comes to me. I trust in God's heavenly plan for happiness. The Holy Spirit breathes deep love, deep happiness, and deep abundance in me and fills me. I am grateful for this journey. I am love. I am loved.

– FEEL

Trusting is my strength. God has a plan for heavenly happiness. I can only trust in God's plan.

What am I here to learn? I surrender to my purpose of staying connected to my heart. My vulnerability is my shield. My feelings are my best friends. My feelings are my guide. I am here for myself. I am here to feel my emotions. My energy is my strength. Why should I trust? I take care of me. I take care of my heart. My loving presence is my gift to others. I don't understand. It's not for me to understand. Showing up for myself is my strength. My confidence comes from staying connected to my heart. I will be okay. I am soft, sacred feminine energy. I honor myself. I honor my feminine beauty. I am grateful for this journey. I am a receiver of good energy. The Holy Spirit fills me with deep love, deep happiness, and deep abundance. Abundance flows to me easily and effortlessly every day. I am magnetic energy. I attract everything I desire. I am worthy of attracting financial abundance.

– TRUST

My strength is my feminine energy. I am magnetic energy. Everything will be okay. My true value as a woman is my energy. I trust in God's heavenly plan for happiness. Everything is always working out for me. There must be value in this.

What am I here to learn? My pain is my strength. Trusting is my confidence. My truth is my loving presence. My gift is my loving presence. Where do I not trust myself? I am attracting everything I desire. I am here for me. I am committed to myself. I am the only one who can take care of me the way I truly need. Setting goals and taking steps moves me forward. I am grateful for this journey. I will show up because that's my gift. I am full of life. I regenerate deep love, deep happiness, and deep abundance over and over again. The Holy Spirit fills me up. I am blessed. I am grateful. Jesus holds my hand. I am trusting everything is always working out for me.

– ACCEPTANCE

What am I here to learn? What am I afraid of? My heart is full. Staying small is so much easier. The Holy Spirit fills me with deep love, deep joy, and deep abundance. I'm afraid. Trusting is my strength. I am magnetic energy. Everything is always working out for me. I am beautiful. My soft, sacred energy is regenerating over and over. I accept where I am. I am making peace with where I am. Everything is attracted to me because of how I feel inside. I am a magnet for positive energy. I am grateful. I'm creating everything I desire. I am worthy of everything I desire. I am soft, sacred feminine energy. I am love. I love myself. I give myself permission to give love and receive love freely. Abundance flows easily and effortlessly to me every single day. I'm here for a reason. I don't understand. I don't need to understand. Letting go and allowing is my feminine energy, and this is my strength. I trust in God's heavenly plan for happiness and love.

91

– RECEIVE

Holding my pain is my strength. Having compassion on my pain gives me confidence. God has a plan for me. I am blessed. My life is a gift. This journey is a gift. I don't understand. I don't need to understand. My masculine energy is my discipline. What does my masculine energy want from me? I need to listen. I don't need to be in control. Surrendering to my purpose of staying connected to my heart is my strength. I don't have to do a single thing to prove myself. Receiving is my strength. Trusting is my strength. I accept where I am. My heart is open. Feeling every experience and every pain makes me deeper. Everything is always working out for me. I believe in my value. My power comes from my loving heart. I am me. I love me. I am grateful. I am worthy of abundance. Receiving and trusting is my strength. God will show me what it is I am to receive. I am ready to receive. Everything I desire in my life will come to me. I am open to receiving the Holy Spirit filling me up with deep love, deep joy, and deep abundance. I am love.

WEEK 24

– EMPOWERMENT

Staying neutral is hard. My feminine energy is my confidence. I'm experiencing so much regret. I need to center myself in my heart. Feeling bad doesn't serve me. I am okay. Everything will be okay. I am magnetic energy. I can handle anything that comes my way. My focus is my energy. Staying connected in my body is my strength. My empowered life comes from inside of me. I am a forgiven child of God. I forgive myself. I don't know how to control my emotions. My loving presence is my greatest gift. I am grateful for this journey.

What am I here to learn? Letting go and trusting gives me more strength.

– FEEL

What am I here to learn? I am attracting everything I want. I deserve everything I desire. What am I feeling? I am becoming deeper because I am more afraid than ever. My heart is open. I am open to receiving. My feminine energy is my strength. My power is my energy. I am dynamic. I radiate deep love and deep abundance. The Holy Spirit regenerates fullness through me over and over again. I am going to be okay. I'm still afraid. I trust in God's plan for happiness. None of this is my plan. I am okay. I am healing. Living moment to moment is my strength. I am grateful for this journey. I love myself. It's okay to love me. I am here to take care of me. I show up every morning because I love myself and I take care of myself. No one can take care of me better than I can. The Holy Spirit radiates love, joy, and abundance through me. I am a forgiven child of God. I surrender to my purpose of staying connected to my heart.

– TRUST

What am I here to learn? My pain is my strength. I am becoming a deeper energy. I trust in God's heavenly plan for happiness. I can trust any situation that comes my way. Everything is always working out for me. I don't understand. I am trusting life and that everything is working out for me. There must be value in this. My pain is my strength. What is my vulnerability? My heart is a deep, loving soul. I surrender to my purpose of staying connected to my heart. My heart is open. I love myself. I trust myself. My confidence comes from trusting. I'm afraid. I'm sad. I don't want to be disappointed. My heart hurts. I am here for me. I show up for me. I am the only one who can take care of me the way I desire. I am worthy of abundance. Abundance flows to me easily and effortlessly every single day. I have no plan. I am soft, sacred feminine energy. I am love. I am beautiful feminine energy. My vulnerability is my strength. I love myself. Trusting is my strength. This is my true power. I am grateful for this journey. Letting go is my strength. My power is feeling my pain. My softness and gentleness are my gift. My loving presence is my gift.

What am I here to learn? My soft gentleness is my strength as a woman. The Holy Spirit fills me with deep love, deep joy, and deep abundance.

– ACCEPTANCE

I am committed to me and my success. I deserve abundance. I deserve happiness. I deserve my dream life. I tend to my own energy first. I attract abundance. The Holy Spirit fills me up. I trust in God's heavenly plan. I trust and allow good things to happen to me. I trust that everything is working the way it's supposed to. The problems in my life are solving themselves. I am excited to be on this journey. Everything is okay. I am full of feminine energy. I am dynamic. I am beautiful. I am attractive. I am love. I am joy. I am regenerating only positive energy. I am the creator of my happiness and everything I desire. I allow only good energy in my life. I am soft, feminine energy. I am worthy of abundance. I acknowledge my heart. I acknowledge my true wisdom. I am grateful. I am healing. I am comfortable making myself vulnerable. This is my strength. This is my confidence. I am grateful for this journey and who I have become. I am taking care of me. My heart is open. I am confident with who I am. I only allow good things to flow through my life. I trust in God's heavenly plan for peace and happiness.

– RECEIVE

What am I here to learn? I am worthy of receiving only positive energy. My value is my feminine energy. My energy is valuable. I am a receiver of good energy. Abundance flows to me easily and effortlessly every day. I trust in God's heavenly plan. I trust in God's plan for happiness here on earth. I love myself. I am here to take care of me. I am love. My heart is love. I surrender to my purpose of staying connected to my heart and my feminine energy. I value myself. I am a high-value woman. I am worthy of everything I desire. I am ready to receive everything I desire. I have an abundance mindset. Everything is okay. Everything is working out for me. My feminine energy is magnetic. I am soft, sacred feminine energy. The Holy Spirit fills me up and regenerates my heart with love, joy, and abundance. I don't understand. I don't need to understand. I hold compassion for myself. I forgive myself as God forgives me. I am a receiver, and that is truly my gift. My loving presence is magnetic. I believe in me. I love me.

WEEK 25

– EMPOWERMENT

Trusting is my strength. Everything is always working out for me. Staying connected to my body empowers me. Inspiration comes from my heart. I show up for myself. I am here for me. My feminine energy is my true power. Feeling the world through my feminine energy builds my confidence. My true value comes from me. Experiencing every moment allows me to stay in my feminine energy.

My vulnerability is my strength. Everything I desire is attracted to me just because of who I am. Staying out of my head is my strength. My power comes from dropping down into my heart. My loving presence is my gift. I can handle with grace anything that comes my way. Staying connected to my physical self allows me to attract everything I need. Being still and closing my eyes allows the energy inside of me to move into my true feminine center. Getting inside of every moment pulls the whole world towards me.

– FEEL

I am committed to myself. I am committed to my success. I believe in my success. Others believe in me. I am passionate about becoming successful. My pain is bringing me closer and closer to my truth. I am grateful for my journey. I deserve happiness. I deserve abundance. Abundance is simply energy. I am not afraid of that energy. Abundance is here to serve me. I am grateful. I am radiant. I am attractive. I am worthy of abundance. I trust in God's heavenly plan. My confidence comes from my heart. The Holy Spirit fills me up. My heart is full of happiness. I deserve happiness. I attract happiness. I attract good energy. Everything is working out the way it's supposed to be. My heart is open. My power is my energy. I choose to be happy. I am authentic. I am afraid to make myself vulnerable. My intention is to feel with my heart. All of my love comes from my heart. My purpose is to stay connected to my heart.

– TRUST

What am I here to learn? What question should I be asking that I don't already know. I am so grateful for this journey. My feminine energy is my confidence. My energy is what makes me who I am. I am positive energy. I am soft, sacred feminine energy. My fear is a sign for me that this is growth. Being scared means I'm not embracing growth. I trust in God's plan for happiness. My pain makes me stronger. I trust everything is always working out for me. Trusting is the best solution. Abundance flows to me easily and effortlessly every day. I am worthy of abundance. I am worthy of everything I desire. I am attracting abundance. The Holy Spirit fills my heart with deep love, deep happiness, and deep abundance. My gift to others is to be fully present. My strength is showing up. I haven't shown up for myself in the past. It's time to show up for me and to take care of my heart and soul. I trust everything is always working out for me. I show up for me. I am trustworthy. My vulnerability and transparency are my strength. I am committed to myself. That's how I build trust.

– ACCEPTANCE

I am here for me. I am here to listen to my heart. I am grateful for learning this. I am amazing. I am attractive. I am beautiful. I deserve abundance. I am so grateful. I trust in God's heavenly plan. I am a happy and strong kind person. I am attracting abundance. My purpose is my heart. Good things in every area of my life come to me. I deserve to receive abundance. I am not in control. God has more planned for me than I can ever imagine. I am attracting abundance. I am excited to be on this journey. I am in a state of allowing. Everything is okay, and I am growing. I am dynamic, and I am regenerating love and happiness and energy. I am attracting what I am creating inside of me. My true power as a woman is knowing that I deserve everything that comes my way. I am worthy of receiving abundance. I am filled with the Holy Spirit.

– RECEIVE

I am a good receiver. Trusting is my strength. I don't understand. I don't have to do anything to be valuable. I have compassion on my heart. I am very valuable energy. What does surrender mean? By trusting I surrender. I want happiness. Staying in my feminine energy makes me magnetic. Receiving is feminine energy. I am valuable. I am a high-value woman. Nothing I do or say alters my value. Seeing myself as a beautiful person is magnetic. My worth comes from my energy inside of me. I value myself as a high-value woman. Letting go is my strength. I'm sad because I have to make myself happy. I am grateful for this journey. My heart is so full of love. I radiate deep love, deep radiance, deep abundance. I have access to all the energy I'll ever need. The Holy Spirit radiates in me over and over again. My confidence comes from my heart. Taking care of me is my feminine energy. Trusting is my strength. Staying in my feminine energy is my strength. I was brought into this world for love. I've always been angry. I've always been scared. Nothing has ever been good enough. I think I found the missing link in my life, but it's turned my life upside down. I've found more confidence and feel the burning desire.

WEEK 26

– EMPOWERMENT

What am I here to learn? I have fear. My power is in my body, not my head. My head hurts. How do I get out of my head? Overthinking and over-analyzing does not serve me. Empowerment comes when I feel confidence and feel steady with myself. I can handle anything with grace that comes my way. I am magnetic energy. Staying connected with my body helps me be more empowered. I know my true inner wisdom comes from my body. Feeling my energy is where my true power lies. I surrender to staying connected to my heart. I forgive myself. Going within and getting into my body allows me to get into my true feminine power. Getting inside of every moment is feminine energy. Everything is always working out for me. There is a reason for me to learn this lesson. I make mistakes. That's who I am. I am finding me. I am soft, healing energy. My inner energy inside of my body is my true power. What am I feeling?

What am I here to learn? Why is this happening? I'm so afraid. Why do I keep making mistakes? I'm embarrassed. How do I forgive myself? I am a good person. I deserve happiness. I deserve abundance. I am happier than ever. I like people, and they like me.

– FEEL

I trust in God's plan for heavenly happiness. My feelings deserve love.

What am I here to learn? This is all about learning how to trust. What am I feeling? Everything is always working out for me. I deserve deep love and deep abundance. My confidence comes from my feelings. I surrender to my purpose of staying connected to my heart. I am open to myself. My heart is open. My power is in my energy. I am dynamic. I radiate love. I am authentic. My pain is my strength. My feelings are my power. Taking care of myself is my strength. Only I can take care of me the way I crave. I honor myself. I honor my feelings.

– TRUST

I trust myself. I trust in God's heavenly plan. I trust everything is always working out for me. Trusting is my strength. I am grateful for this journey. I am worthy of abundance. Abundance flows to me easily and effortlessly every day. My vulnerability is my strength. It is my shield. My transparency is my shield. It's my right to receive everything I desire. I surrender to staying connected to my heart, which is my purpose. My loving presence is my gift to the world. My soft, sacred feminine energy is my gift. My heart is love.

– ACCEPTANCE

Trusting and allowing is my strength. My greatest power is receiving inspiration from the Holy Spirit. I am attracting everything I want towards me. Everything is always working out for me. I trust in God's heavenly plan for happiness. I am a full, dynamic woman. I am attracting fullness. I am radiant. I allow only positive energy. Facing my fears is my strength.

What am I here to learn? I am a soft, sacred feminine vessel. My true power as a woman is my feeling center. I am grateful for this journey. I trust my heart. The Holy Spirit gives me strength and fills me up. I surrender to staying connected to my heart. That is my purpose. Abundance flows to me easily and effortlessly every day. I only feel love. I am grateful for the deep love I feel. My plan is not as beautiful as the one God has planned for me. I trust in God's deep love for me.

– RECEIVE

What am I here to learn? My ability to neutralize allows me to receive. I am a receiver of good energy. I am worthy of receiving deep love, deep happiness, and deep abundance. I am the holder of valuable sacred, soft energy. The Holy Spirit fills me up and regenerates energy inside of me over and over again. My heart is open. I am love. I am loving. I am loved. I am a good receiver. Being present and experiencing every moment fills me up and makes me more magnetic. I am a receiver of good positive energy. My loving presence is a gift. I believe in my value. My value comes from my loving heart. This is my truth. I believe I am a beautiful heart. I am a high-value woman. Staying connected to my heart is where my value lies. I deserve high-value relationships. I am worthy of abundance because of who I am. I am open to receiving from myself and from life. I surrender to my purpose of staying connected to my heart. I deserve happiness. I take care of me. Inspiration breathes through me. I am full of love, life, and light. I naturally radiate this energy. I am deep love, deep happiness, and deep abundance. My vulnerability makes me stronger. My heart knows the truth. I am aligned with my heart and my truth. I am life. I radiate life. My good health is a bi-product of my soft, sacred energy.

WEEK 27

– EMPOWERMENT

What am I here to learn? I am an elevated sacred, soft, feminine energy. My intuition knows. My power and energy lie in my body. My self-confidence comes from my feminine power. Everything I desire is being attracted to me. The feelings I am experiencing make me stronger. I can handle with grace anything that comes my way. Staying connected to my body helps me connect to my inner wisdom. I am pulling the whole world towards me. Taking care of my energy is what matters most. Every day I keep my body moving, which allows me to experience how I feel. My feelings are valid. I acknowledge I am experiencing these feelings. I feel these feelings not only in my mind, but in my body.

My empowered life does not come from the exterior world. Going within helps me step into my true power. My embodiment comes from slowing down and experiencing the moment. Getting inside of every moment pulls the world towards me. My feminine energy is a magnetic field that I feel throughout my body. I deserve abundance. I am worthy of deep love, deep joy, and deep abundance. I trust in God's plans for earthly and heavenly happiness.

– FEEL

I love myself. My feminine energy is magnetic. I protect myself. I am here to take care of me. I am the only one who can take care of me the way I feel I deserve. I surrender to my purpose of staying connected to my heart. I trust in God's heavenly plan for happiness. My feminine energy is my strength. Trusting is my strength. My confidence comes from trusting myself. Everything I desire comes from within me. Everything is okay. Everything is working out the way God has planned. I am here to enjoy the journey. The Holy Spirit fills me up. My pain and the love I feel in my heart make me stronger. These feelings make me a deeper person. My energy is my power. I am dynamic. My beauty comes from my heart. I am authentic. I'm afraid. My heart hurts. I'm still afraid. I don't like being scared. I don't like running. I trust in God's heavenly plan. I don't need to understand.

Trusting is my strength. I am grounded in myself. I protect my heart. I don't want to be abandoned. I am inspired. My love gives me strength to stay within my boundaries. I love myself. I am love. I am loving. I am loved. I surrender to my purpose. Staying connected to my heart is my vulnerability. I trust in God's heavenly plan for happiness. I am grateful for this journey. I am brave. My gift to others is my loving presence. I trust myself. I know what to do.

– TRUST

I am here for myself. I show up for myself. I trust in God's plan for happiness. Everything is always working out for me. My true value is trusting.

What am I here to learn? I trust myself. My heart is open. I trust life. There must be value in this. There must be value in my feelings. I trust my intuition. My pain is my strength. I surrender to my purpose of staying connected to my heart. My vulnerability is my strength. Where have I not trusted myself in the past? Keeping my commitments to myself is how I trust myself. Taking care of my heart builds my confidence. How do I take care of me? I take care of my heart by honoring my commitments. I love myself. I take care of myself. I show up for myself. What am I here to observe? Can I observe my breath? My breathing comes naturally. I don't have to force it. I am loved. I am filled with deep joy, deep love, and deep abundance. The Holy Spirit regenerates soft, sacred feminine energy inside of me over and over again. I am love. It is my right to receive everything I desire. Love flows from my heart. My true power comes from inside of me. My vulnerability is my power and my gift to the world. My power is not in protecting myself. My loving presence is my greatest gift. I cherish myself and my loving energy. My true power as a woman is my soft, sacred feminine energy.

– ACCEPTANCE

What am I here to learn? I am here to trust God's heavenly plan. I am attracting positive energy and abundance into my life. My confidence comes from my heart. The Holy Spirit fills me up with deep love and deep abundance. I am grateful for this journey. I surrender to God's plan. I am ready to receive. I am attracting everything I desire. I am a receiver of good energy. Everything is working out the way it's supposed to. Everything is okay.

What am I here to learn? I am strong. I will be okay. I am here for me. I take care of my loving heart. I love myself. I am worthy of abundance. Finding my feminine energy is where I will find my confidence. Only I can love me the way I desire. Trusting is my strength. I am worthy of everything I desire. I deserve abundance. My vulnerability is my strength. I surrender to my purpose of staying connected to my heart. I am content with who I am. I am soft, sacred feminine energy.

– RECEIVE

The Holy Spirit breathes positive energy into me. I am a receiver of good energy. I receive good energy because of who I am. How do I stay in alignment with myself? I have compassion for me. I forgive myself. I am a good receiver.

What am I here to learn? I am a high-value woman. I have a loving heart and a wise soul. I am a beautiful person. I am worthy of high-level energy. My worth comes from what I feel inside. I am worthy of good things. My pain and fear are my strength.

What am I here to learn? Everything I desire in life I am worthy of receiving. I am grounded in my feminine energy.

WEEK 28

– EMPOWERMENT

I am feminine energy. I trust in God's heavenly plan. My confidence comes from my heart. Empowerment comes when I anchor myself in my body. I am attracting everything I need in my life. I am magnetic energy. I am soft, sacred feminine energy. I am here for me. I show up for myself. My true power comes from my heart. I surrender to my purpose of staying connected to my heart. Getting inside of every moment allows me to get inside of my body.

Everything I desire is naturally attracted to me. My truth is inside my heart. My loving presence is my gift to the world. What am I experiencing? What am I feeling? My power and energy are in my body and not in my head. Staying centered in my heart brings me my confidence. I don't understand. I don't want to understand. I can handle with grace anything that comes my way. Staying connected to my body helps me attract everything I want in the world. Staying grounded in my body is my magnetic energy. Getting into my head doesn't serve me. I am true to me.

– FEEL

I take care of me. My loving presence is my gift to others. I attract positive energy. I am fully present for myself.

What am I here to learn? I attract abundance. Trusting is where I find strength. I trust in God's heavenly plan. Everything is always working out for me. I am dynamic. I radiate deep love. I am authentic. I only want to attract people who love me. I love myself. I'm afraid of being lonely. Jesus holds my hand. The Holy Spirit fills me up and regenerates deep energy over and over again. I take care of my heart. I love myself. I am love. I am elevated energy. I am soft and sacred feminine energy. Trusting is feminine energy. My heart is magnetic. I only attract positive energy and energy that fills me up. I am worthy of abundance. I am worthy of God's love. I am a forgiven child of God. I am grateful for this journey and for finding myself. There's nothing I can do to change anything. I release or surrender the illusion of control. I am here to receive. I honor myself. I honor my feminine energy. Everything is always working out for me. I deserve abundance. I am worthy of good energy.

– TRUST

My heart is love. I am always scared.

What am I here to learn? I surrender to my purpose of staying connected to my heart. My confidence comes from my heart. My soft, sacred energy is magnetic. I believe I am worthy. I believe I am sacred. I trust in God's heavenly plan for happiness. Trusting in God's plan is my strength. My transparency and vulnerability are my connection to others. My pain gives me deep love, deep happiness, and deep abundance. I am grateful for this journey. I will be okay. Everything is always working out for me. Trusting is my strength. My loving presence is my gift to others. I am here for me. I trust myself. I take care of my heart. I love myself. I value myself. I am becoming a deeper soul. I can handle everything that comes my way. My true power comes from trusting that everything is working out for me. My pain and suffering bring me to my higher truth. I am trustworthy. I keep my commitments to myself. I heal myself from the inside out. My trust in myself builds trust with others. I cherish myself. I radiate soft, sacred feminine energy. I have an abundance mindset. Abundance flows to me.

– ACCEPTANCE

What am I here to learn? Staying in my feminine energy is where I find my confidence. My heart is full of love. Everything is always working out for me. Receiving inspiration from the Holy Spirit brings me life. I am grateful for this journey. I trust in God's plan for heavenly happiness. I don't need to understand. My energy is full of deep love, deep joy, and deep abundance. The Holy Spirit is guiding me. I am a fluid, dynamic energy that is regenerating fullness over and over again. My heart is full of deep love, deep joy, and deep happiness. I am at peace with who I am and with where I am. I choose to feel abundance. My greatest power is feeling every emotion. I don't have to have a plan. I am already everything that I desire. My pain is my strength. Staying transparent and vulnerable makes me stronger and more magnetic. I am worthy of everything I want. My fears mean I'm growing. My journey is about finding my confidence. I don't understand, but I don't need to understand. I love myself. I take care of my loving heart. I take care of me.

How can I allow my true intuition into my heart?

– RECEIVE

I am a receiver of good energy. I value myself. I am worthy of everything I desire. I am magnetic feminine energy. My heart is open. I am beautiful valuable energy. This is where my true value lies. I am a receiver of good energy. My loving presence is my gift to others. There is nothing I have to do to prove myself. I am a good listener. I am always a receiver. I am stepping into my power and am fully receiving. As I realize my value, I become a high-value woman. I believe in my value. I have a loving heart and a wise soul. I feel my sense of worth. My sense of worth is where my value lies. I trust in God's heavenly plan for happiness. Everything is always working out for me. The Holy Spirit fills me up with deep love, deep happiness, and deep abundance. I attract only positive energy. I am worthy of positive energy. I deserve abundance. I am a receiver of abundance. Jesus holds my hand. My strength comes from my magnetic center which attracts everything I desire. I am so full of love and light that I can't help but naturally radiate this beauty. I am soft, sacred feminine energy. Everything I desire naturally flows to me because I radiate inside.

WEEK 29

– EMPOWERMENT

I am growing my garden of abundance. The seeds are planted for me to live the life I desire.

What am I here to learn? What am I feeling? What is my body telling me? I can handle anything with grace. I am attracting everything I need in life. I am pulling the whole world to me. Finding myself creates my empowered life. I need me to show up for me. I am committed to me. I am grateful for this journey. I am love. I am loving. I am loved. I am soft, sacred feminine energy. I am worthy of abundance. The seeds have been planted. I am growing and nurturing myself. My transparency and vulnerability are my strength. I am healing. I don't understand. I don't need to understand. I am grateful for this journey. I am the only one who can take care of me.

What am I here to learn? I am trustworthy because I show up for me. I attract everything I desire.

– FEEL

Showing up for myself gives me confidence.

What am I here to learn? I love myself. My heart is open. I surrender to my purpose of staying connected to my heat. My vulnerability makes me stronger. I am dynamic energy. I am the receiver of good energy. I trust in God's plan for happiness. I am becoming a deeper soul. I am soft, sacred energy. I radiate abundance. I am authentic. I am healing. I am grateful for journey. Staying connected to my heart is where I find my confidence. I am building a stronger connection with my heart. I am magnetic. My heart holds all my feelings. My heart heals me. I am worthy of abundance. I am worthy of positive energy. My inner strength is part of my beauty. My deep feelings make me stronger every day. I am deep love, deep joy, and deep happiness. I attract everything I desire. Everything will be okay. I grow stronger every day.

– TRUST

I show up for me. I trust myself. I trust life. I trust in God's plan. My value and my worth come from within me. My true value and worth as a woman come from my heart. I am becoming a deeper soul. I can handle anything. Everything is always working out for me.

What am I here to learn? I trust my intuition. My vulnerability is my strength. I am a beautiful loving feminine energy. I surrender to my purpose of staying connected to my heart. Trusting is my strength. Where do I not trust myself? Where am I not being authentic? Where am I not being aligned? I am committed to myself. I am committed to my business and working on things that make me feel good. As I become more trusting in myself, I become more trustworthy. I am soft, sacred feminine energy. My pain is my strength. I love myself. I am compassionate with me. My gentleness and vulnerability are my shield. My transparency is my protection. I am worthy of everything I desire. My true power is my heart. My soft vulnerability floods my body. My power is not in protecting myself. My power is feeling into my vulnerability. My loving presence is my gift to others. I cherish myself. The Holy Spirit fills me with deep love, deep happiness, and deep abundance. I love who I am. I protect myself. I take care of me.

– ACCEPTANCE

My true power is my magnetic energy. I am soft, sacred feminine energy. My loving presence is my gift to others. I am worthy of deep love, deep joy, and deep abundance. Abundance flows to me easily and effortlessly every single day. I am worthy of abundance. My heart is open. I am love. **How does my mindset match with my purpose? Is my mindset moving me forward with my purpose?**

– RECEIVE

What am I here to learn? I don't understand. I don't need to understand. What does it mean to receive? I surrender to my heart. I surrender to my purpose of staying connected to my heart. My worthiness lies in my energy. My energy is my gift to others. My true power is when I bring others into my heart. I am the beholder of beautiful energy. This is my true power. The Holy Spirit regenerates deep love, deep joy, and deep abundance inside of me. I don't need to prove myself to anybody. I need to take care of my heart. Receiving is my strength. I am fully present when stepping into my power, and I experience every moment. Every experience makes me who I am. I deserve to receive good energy. I am valuable. I believe in my value. I am a loving heart. I am a beautiful person. I attract abundance. I am worthy of everything I desire. My truth is in my heart. I am open to receiving. What am I here to receive? I am afraid to receive. Trusting is my strength. Everything I create comes from inside of me. What am I willing to receive? I am magnetic energy receiving positive energy. I radiate this energy.

WEEK 30

– EMPOWERMENT

I am expanding. I am becoming more of who I am. What am I here to learn? What am I holding onto? What am I willing to not let go or what am I not willing to let go? I make myself happy. What am I feeling? My power exists in my body and in my heart. Trusting is my strength. I can handle with grace anything that comes my way. I'm learning. I'm afraid. Feeling is my strength. Staying in my body is where I'll find my confidence. Slowing down and experiencing is feminine energy. Staying in my body helps me experience my energy. How do I stay in my energy? Feeling my energy is my strength. Is it possible to ask myself over and over what am I feeling? How do I truly stay grounded in myself? What can I do to feel my essence? I am still finding myself? Staying grounded is my feminine energy. What can I do every moment to stay grounded? How do I let go of my thinking? I don't' understand.

What am I here to learn? I am love.

– FEEL

I am okay. Everything is always working out for me. My family is my priority. I am soft, sacred feminine energy. I only need to be myself. My loving presence is my gift to others. I trust in God's heavenly plan for happiness. I surrender to my purpose of staying connected to my heart. I am attracting abundance in my life. The Holy Spirit fills me with deep love, deep happiness, and deep abundance. I attract only positive energy. My feelings are my power. My embarrassment makes me stronger. My feelings are my best friends. My feelings are my guide. My feelings teach me. Only I am in control of my feelings. If I'm embarrassed, it is okay.

What am I here to learn? Everything is okay. I am becoming fuller of who I am. I'm not afraid. My fear makes me stronger. My feelings are a power place. Trusting is my strength. I don't need a plan. I don't need to understand. I am dynamic energy. I radiate beauty. Walking into my pain and experiencing it fully makes me stronger. My deeper feelings help me find what I've given away. I have compassion for myself. I protect my heart. My inner strength is part of my beauty. I am grateful for this journey. I honor my feminine energy. By honoring my energy, I honor myself. I honor my feelings.

– TRUST

I trust myself. I show up for me. I trust in God's heavenly plan. Everything is always working out for me. I trust the future.

What am I here to learn? My deeper soul allows me to handle everything. My true power comes from trusting myself. If everything is working out for me, there must be value in this. My body and feelings have all the answers. My heart is where my confidence lies. I am healing. I am beautiful, confident energy. My heart is open. I trust myself. I'm worthy of deep love, deep happiness, and deep abundance. I am committed to myself. I show up for me. I take care of my heart. I am what matters most. As I become more trusting in myself, I become more trusting in my relationships. Acknowledging all of my feelings brings me into my heart. I take care of myself. I love myself. I have compassion for myself when my heart hurts. I am full of love. Staying connected to my heart is my purpose. My vulnerability is my strength. It's my right to experience and receive everything I desire. My transparency is my shield. My true power is my sensitivity. My power is not in protecting myself. My softness and gentleness are my gift. My true power, as a woman, is my heart.

– ACCEPTANCE

My heart is open. I am love. I am loving. Trusting is my strength. Everything is always working out for me. I am a receiver of positive energy. The Holy Spirit regenerates deep love, deep joy, and deep abundance over and over and over and over again. I surrender to my purpose of staying connected to my heart. I am attracting abundance into my life. I trust in God's plan for happiness. Everything is okay. I take care of myself and my loving heart. I am a full, fluid dynamic feminine energy. I only come from a state of fullness. My heart is full. I attract everything to me that I desire. I am at peace with myself. I show up for me.

What am I here to learn? I am what I think. I shift over to a positive mindset. Everything I desire I already have inside of me. I attract everything I desire. I am full of positive energy. I am the creator of everything I desire. My fear means I'm growing. I love myself. I take care of myself. My heart is full of positive energy. My masculine energy protects me. I am so grateful for this journey. I am finding myself. Whatever I am, I am on the inside. No one externally can change who I am. I am worthy of everything I desire. Abundance flows to me easily and effortlessly every single day. I am above chasing. I only attract. I am warm, loving energy. My loving presence is my greatest gift to the world. I can only be me.

– RECEIVE

What am I here to learn? I am worthy of receiving everything I desire. My feminine energy is my gift. Bringing people into my heart is my gift to others. I am a receiver of good energy. I have an abundance mindset. I am grateful for this journey. I am a grateful receiver. I realize how valuable I am. I am anchored in my truth. I am worthy of receiving everything I desire. I can handle everything that comes my way. I am worthy of everything I desire because of who I am. I take care of myself. I take care of my heart. Everything I desire comes from what I create inside of me. I am good enough. I want to be a good receiver. I am good enough. I take care of those I love.

WEEK 31

– EMPOWERMENT

I am ready to receive everything God has planned for me. I am manifesting everything I desire. I am here to be at peace with everything. I am here to experience what life wants me to feel. My feminine power is my confidence. I surrender to my feminine energy. I am anchored in my nervousness. My breath anchors me. My nervousness empowers me. I am manifesting everything I desire. I surrender to being me. I am grateful for this journey. I am me—and I can only be me. My fear makes me stronger.

My power comes from my nervousness. I have been given a gift, and I am grateful. Slowing down and experiencing this nervousness brings out my strength. Jesus holds my hand. The Holy Spirit fills me with deep joy, deep happiness, and deep abundance. All of my strength comes from inside of me. I make myself happy. I am my strength. My pain is my strength. I am growing, and I am healing.

Everything God has planned for me is better than I can ever imagine. Everything I need is inside me. I think I understand, but I don't understand. My heart tells me to trust. But I don't like the pain. How can I let go of the pain? I am so grateful for this journey. I wouldn't have found myself if I wouldn't have gone through this pain. I accept where I am. I can't change anything. I can only be me. Feeling my nervousness is my confidence. Trusting is God's plan. I am feminine energy, and I feel the pain. I am manifesting everything I desire because I am worthy of receiving abundance.

– FEEL

What am I here to learn? I am grateful for this journey. I am worthy of abundance. My fear means growth. Staying cut off from my feelings shuts me off from my intuition. Feeling the deeper feelings make me stronger. Feeling the deeper feelings keeps me out of my head. It helps me experience my own life so others can experience me through my feeling source. My feelings are the indicator if things are going well or if I'm not on the right track. My feelings are my amazing super power. Staying open to my feelings and to the world allows me to know if things are going well. The more I understand my feelings and emotions helps me attract the energy I deserve. My feelings are my power place. Staying connected to my heart is my strength. I honor myself. I protect my heart. Trusting is my strength. My heart is full. My heart is open. I don't understand. I don't need to understand. God has a plan, and I will trust that everything is always working out for me.

– TRUST

Where don't I trust myself? Trusting God is my strength. I trust in God's heavenly plan for happiness. I trust the future. Whatever lies ahead I can trust. Stepping into my power makes me a deeper soul. Everything I desire is working out for me.

What am I here to learn? There must be value in this. My vulnerability is my strength. I am a deeper person. Trusting myself is where it all starts. Keeping my commitments to myself are my top priority. Keeping my commitments to myself helps me trust myself. I am learning to love myself. Loving me is what matters most. My softness and gentleness are a gift. The Holy Spirit enlightens me with my true power. My vulnerability and my sensitivity are my strength. I cherish myself. My power is not in protecting myself. My power is not being afraid to show my vulnerability. I am grateful for my feminine energy. Gentleness and love keep me connected to my feminine energy. I surrender to my purpose of staying connected to my heart.

– ACCEPTANCE

What am I here to learn? What if I am wrong? What if this isn't the answer? I surrender to God's plan. Trusting is all I have. My feminine energy is my magnetic power. Abundance is energy which is attracted to me. Everything is working the way it's supposed to. Everything is okay. This is an opportunity for me to learn a new lesson. The Holy Spirit fills me with deep love, deep happiness, and deep abundance. My feminine energy regenerates over and over again. I attract everything I create inside of me. I am grateful for this journey. My heart is open. I surrender to my purpose of staying connected to my heart. My vulnerability and transparency are my strength. I am worthy of everything I desire. God has a plan for me which is better than anything I can create. I am worthy of everything that comes my way. I deserve positive energy. I am a forgiven child of God. I trust in God's plan. I will hold Jesus' hand. I know everything in abundance is being attracted to me.

– RECEIVE

My value is not what I do or give to others. My value is my energy. I am worthy of anything I desire. My feminine energy is my gift others. Jesus holds my hand. I am the holder of beautiful valuable energy. I am grateful for this journey. The Holy Spirit fills me with deep love. I am valuable because of who I am. I am sacred, soft, feminine energy. My vulnerability is my shield. I am a receiver of good energy. I am a high-value woman. My core value comes from inside of me. I am worthy of receiving only high-level energy. Staying elevated is my strength. I am worthy of everything I desire because of who I am. I want to find myself. I want to find joy in my heart. The true joy I'm looking for is inside of me. I'm learning that true joy doesn't come from anything outside of me. True joy comes from inside my heart. I am worthy of true joy. My heart is open to receiving true joy. My happiness and my joy come from deep inside of me. My pain is healing me. I am God's child. I trust in God's plan for heavenly happiness one day. My true value is my energy inside of me.

WEEK 32

– EMPOWERMENT

I am experiencing pain. I am healthy and I heal myself. I am grateful. I am ready to step away from the pain. I am empowered by staying centered in my body. I am pulling the whole world to my magnetic energy. My energy is misaligned. I need to figure out why I'm feeling so off. Trusting gives me courage.

My empowered life originates from my inner energy. I love me. I am here to love me. I am experiencing pain and loneliness. What am I here to learn by slowing down and experiencing this pain? Feeling pain hurts too much. My inner child doesn't want this pain. I don't like the pain. Why am I not happy? Surrendering is my only strength. I'm afraid. What am I afraid of? What is my truth? I am grateful. I surrender to my truth of staying connected to the love in my heart. I am me. I am love.

– FEEL

I love myself. I surrender to my purpose of staying connected to my heart. My heart is open. I only attract positive energy. I deserve abundance. I am authentic. I trust in God's heavenly plan. My feelings are a power place. Trusting is my strength. I am an elevated woman and deserve respect and honor. I am not needy. I take care of my feelings. I make all my decisions. I take care of me. I am the only one who knows how to take care of me in the way I truly desire. Can I do this? I love myself. No one loves me more than I love myself. I am love. I am loved. I am loving. I can't take care of anyone but myself. I only attract deep love, deep happiness, and deep abundance.

– TRUST

I am soft, sacred feminine energy. Nothing should be this difficult. I am grateful for this journey. I am becoming better and better every day because I connect with the feminine energy inside of me. I can handle everything that comes my way. I deserve everything in my highest power. I trust everything is always working out for me. There must be value in this. I take care of my heart. I deserve love, respect, and honor. I honor myself. I honor my boundaries. Everything that comes my way helps me step into my higher truth. I surrender to my truth. I surrender to my purpose of staying connected to my heart.

What am I here to learn? Am I ready to trust? Am I ready to be vulnerable? Keeping my commitments to myself is where my trust starts. Showing up for myself builds trust inside of me, which builds trust in my relationships with others. I trust in God's heavenly plan. I am a forgiven child of God. Trusting makes me an elevated woman. I am magnetic. I attract love, joy, and abundance. My vulnerability and sensitivity are my gift to the world. My power is not in protecting myself. My softness and gentleness are a gift to others. I cherish myself and all my insecurities. My true value as a woman is my heart. My soft gentleness is my strength. Staying connected to my heart is my confidence, and it is my purpose. I am who I am because of who I am on the inside.

– ACCEPTANCE

I am attracting everything I want in life. I trust in God's heavenly plan. My vulnerability makes me who I am. Trusting is my strength. I am who I am. I surrender to staying connected to my heart. I show up for me. I am attracting everything I want towards me. My heart is open. Things are always working out for me. I don't understand. I don't need to understand. Showing up is my strength. Everything is okay. This is an opportunity for me to grow. I am a full-fluid dynamic gorgeous body regenerating over and over again. The Holy Spirit fills me with deep love, deep joy, and deep abundance. I am grateful for this journey. I only attract positive energy. My heart is open. The joy I desire is already inside of me. I am the creator of everything I desire. I am soft, sacred feminine energy. I am worthy of everything I want. I am grateful for everything I've been given. I don't understand. I don't need to understand. My loving presence is my gift. I'm afraid. My fear gives me strength. I listen to my heart, not my chatterbox who makes up stories in my head. I am grateful. I will listen to my heart. My soul needs me.

– RECEIVE

I am worthy of receiving abundance. I am manifesting this energy. I am soft, sacred feminine energy. Receiving energy is my gift. I forgive myself. I surrender to my purpose of staying connected to my heart. I believe in my value. I am a loving heart. I am a beautiful person. Everything I desire is coming my way. I am grateful for this journey. I don't understand. I don't need to understand. I trust in God's heavenly plan for happiness. My heart is happy. The Holy Spirit fills my heart with deep love, deep joy, and deep abundance. I am grateful for the Holy Spirit flowing through me. I manifest everything I desire. The universe breathes through me. I understand that I don't need to understand. I surrender to God, who has the answers. I trust in God's plan for happiness. I surrender to receiving God's plan. I am grateful for this journey.

I am divine feminine energy. I am who I am. I am valuable energy worth more than diamonds. I believe in myself. I am building abundance. Everything is okay. Everything is always working out for me. My purpose is my heart. I love myself. I take care of myself. I protect my heart. I am valuable energy. I am here for me. I take care of myself the way no one else can. No one can hurt me or insult me because I take care of me. I am patient.

WEEK 33

– EMPOWERMENT

I am feminine energy. I am worthy of positive energy. My heart is full of gratefulness. I am worthy of abundance, joy, and happiness. I am becoming more of who I am. I embody my feminine energy. I am grateful for this journey. My power comes from my heart. I am anchored in my physical self. I am good enough. I am attracting everything I need in life. I am pulling the whole world to me with my feminine energy. My external world is a reflection of my inner world. Everything will be okay. Everything is always working out for me. I am grateful for this journey. I am pulling the whole world towards me.

– FEEL

Cutting myself off from my feelings doesn't serve me. Distancing myself and running away from my emotions hold me back. What I hide inside of me is what I attract. Facing my emotions head on gives me strength. What am I experiencing right now? My emotions make me stronger and more powerful and deeper in myself. By becoming deeper, I step away from being superficial. I feel deeper. I feel stronger. Facing my painful emotions strengthens my intuition. My feelings are my guide. My feelings help me stay out of my head. Opening up to my feelings 100 percent of the time to myself and to others helps me know what feels good and what I can trust. My power as a woman is to be as authentic as possible. I am not afraid to express all sides of me. My feelings do not shame me. My feelings are my power. Connecting to my physical feelings and my emotional feelings help me become more vulnerable. Facing these emotions help me attract everything I desire in life. By honoring my feelings, I honor myself as deep as they may be.

– TRUST

I honor myself. I have compassion for myself. I surrender to my purpose of staying connected to my heart. I desire honor. I desire happiness. I am compassionate. What is my truth? I am a forgiven child of God. I am grateful for this journey. I am grateful for finding myself. I'm afraid because I don't trust. I am not a victim. I attract only elevated energy. I love myself. I am worthy of honor and compassion. I don't understand. I don't need to understand. I trust in God's timing. I only need to love myself. I am valuable for who I am. I am responsible for my actions. I am available only for my energetic match. I'm only willing to match the same positive energy. Receiving is my strength. I am here to be myself. I only need to be me to attract everything I desire. I don't need to prove myself to anyone. I know I'm beautiful. My beauty is my energy. I can't control anyone. I love myself. I trust myself. I show up for me. I attract matching positive energy. I believe in my value. I am soft, sacred feminine energy. I am love.

– ACCEPTANCE

Trusting is my strength. Showing up for myself keeps me centered. I am full. I feel good. I am in alignment with who I am. I show up for me. I trust everything is always working out for me. I don't understand. I don't need to understand. I soften and surrender to allow what God has in store for me. How do I know I'm in a state of allowing? Knowing the path ahead of me enfolds without me searching for it. The path will find me. I am attracting everything I want towards me, rather than me going out and getting it. Trusting myself and knowing my inspiration come naturally to me. I am grateful for this journey. This is an opportunity for me to grow. I surrender to my purpose of staying connected to my heart. I attract exactly what I'm creating inside of me. I am at peace with where I am right now. I am worthy of abundance. I choose how I feel. I really am what I think. I am positive energy. I am a magnet that attracts positive energy. They Holy Spirit regenerates deep love, deep happiness, and deep abundance in me over and over again. My true power is my feminine energy. Stepping into the feeling of "allowing" steps me into my true power as a woman, knowing that I am worthy of everything that comes my way.

– RECEIVE

I have planted the seeds. I love my life. I trust in God's plan for happiness. I am worthy of everything I desire. My true worth is how I value myself. I am getting comfortable receiving. I believe in my value. I believe I am a high-value woman. I am anchored in my feminine energy. I am worthy of receiving good things. Everything on the outside world matches how I feel on the inside. I am worthy of receiving everything I desire because I am me. I don't need to prove myself to anyone. The universe is excited to give me abundance. I am ready to receive because the seeds have been planted. The Holy Spirit breathes light and love through me. I am divine energy. The Lord provides for me.

WEEK 34

– EMPOWERMENT

What am I here to learn? I am a goddess. I am soft, sacred feminine energy. I am what I feel on the inside. My external world is a reflection of what I feel on the inside. My loving presence is my gift to the world. I love me. I am embodying elevated, feminine energy. I surrender to my purpose of staying connected to my heart. I am magnetic energy, and am manifesting everything I desire.

My energy is my confidence. I love myself. I am worthy of leadership energy. My greatest gift to the world is my loving presence. I am grateful for this journey. I am love. How do I become more of me? Moving out of my head allows me to be more of me. Overthinking doesn't serve me. My self-confidence comes from my heart. Connecting with physical body centers me. Staying centered helps me handle with grace anything that comes my way. My energy grounds me in myself. Everything is naturally attracted to me because I am grounded and anchored in my core values.

My inspired action comes from knowing my truth. Slowing down and experiencing every moment pulls the whole world towards me. Everything I desire naturally comes to me with ease and grace because I am centered in my core values. I am anchored to the moment. I face my fear, I have empathy for all of my emotions. It's okay to feel this way. I honor my truth.

– FEEL

What am I here to learn? This is God's plan. Letting go is helping me become stronger. Life is not for me to control. Life is for me to experience. My transformation is taking time. Being "results oriented" suppresses myself. Letting go allows more of the Holy Spirit to flow through me. My ability to let go and completely surrender takes me on a much bigger journey than I can imagine. I am creating everything in my life. I am not a victim. I am love. I am responsible for what I create. My frequency is empowerment. I don't need to prove myself to anyone. I surrender to my feminine energy. I have the power to create joy in my heart. I have a higher vision for the world. I am not wounded. I have the power to create everything I desire. I am stepping into higher energy. I create positive energy. I deserve positive energy. I don't have control. I don't need to have control. I surrender to my goddess energy. My value is my energy. I don't need to prove myself.

My worth is just being me. Staying focused on my energy inside of me gives me confidence. I love myself. I am not afraid. Everything I desire is attracted to me. I deserve everything I desire. I am worthy of everything I desire. I am amazing. I am warmth and kindness. I am stepping into my highest self. I am the creator of everything in my life. I can do this. My feminine energy is my strength. I am truth. Everything I desire is pulled into my heart. I honor myself. I am grateful for this journey. I trust in God's heavenly plan for love, joy, and abundance. I surrender to God's plan.

– TRUST

I trust that everything will be okay. I am here for me. I show up for me. My value and my worth come from within me. I am becoming a deeper soul. Everything is always working out for me. I am anchored in my inner feelings. My pain is my strength. I surrender to my deeper feelings and my vulnerability. I attract only high-level energy. I attract only positive energy. I am committed to me. I show up for myself every single day. Trusting others comes when I trust myself. As I become more trusting in myself, I become more trusting in my relationships. My power is not in protecting myself. My power is feeling into my vulnerability. My softness and gentleness are my gift and is what is needed around me. I cherish myself. My true power as a woman is my heart. The Holy Spirit fills me up and regenerates deep joy inside of me. I trust in God's plan for happiness.

– ACCEPTANCE

I am becoming more of me. Everything I desire comes from me. I am worthy of receiving abundance. I am soft, sacred feminine energy. The Holy Spirit fills my heart with inspiration. I am committed to myself. I take care of me. I protect myself by allowing and attracting only positive energy. I am worthy of receiving abundance. Connecting deep inside of me allows me to magnify everything I desire. My pain helps go deeper inside of me. I am worthy of receiving because I accept who I truly am. I am so grateful for this journey. I am becoming more of me. Everything I attract is coming because of how I feel inside. The deeper I feel, the more abundance I attract.

– RECEIVE

I am worthy of receiving abundance. I don't have to do anything to be valuable. My loving heart is magnetic energy. I am a receiver of good energy. I trust God's heavenly plan for happiness. I don't understand.

I don't need to understand. I am afraid. I am grateful for this journey. I am worthy of beautiful energy. My heart is open. I am grateful for finding myself. I have found my confidence. My worth is my confidence on the inside. Everything I desire is being attracted to me. I am worthy of everything I desire. I am ready to receive. I am afraid of receiving. I don't know how to receive.

Good things are coming my way and I'm scared. I am beautiful. I am soft, sacred feminine energy. I will be okay. Everything is always working out for me. I surrender to my purpose of staying connected to my heart. The Holy Spirit regenerates love, joy, and abundance inside of me over and over again. My power is my energy inside of me. I own my value. I am divine feminine energy. I bring pure power and pure value to every situation. I am connected to my heart in every single space. I am healing.

WEEK 35

– EMPOWERMENT

I am embodying my feminine energy. I have no control over the future. I can only take care of me. Overthinking doesn't serve me. I can handle with grace anything that comes my way. Staying centered in my body helps me attract abundance. My magnetic energy pulls the whole world towards me. I am, soft, sacred feminine energy. Everything I desire comes from within me. My true power comes from my heart. I surrender to my purpose of staying connected to my heart.

Focusing on my core gives me confidence. I don't like my heart hurting. What am I doing wrong? I honor my soft, sacred feminine energy. My loving presence is my gift to the world. I have an abundance mindset. I am feeling the pain. My pain helps me discover my boundaries. I am worthy of abundance. I will get there by putting myself first, and taking care of me. I am the only one who can show up for me and in the way I want. I am no longer afraid to take care of me. I've hurt myself for too long. The Holy Spirit fills my heart with joy, and I am able to share this joy with others. I am magnetic energy.

– FEEL

What am I here to learn? I've been afraid. Fear drains my energy. Facing my feelings and facing my fears make me who I am. Every time I take on one of my deeper feelings makes me a deeper person. The more I understand the energies in my body amplifies my power as a woman. I am authentic. I am unapologetic for who I am. I only want to attract others who want to understand me. I only attract positive energy. My feelings are a place of power, not a place of shame. Connecting with my own heart first is feminine energy. I am healing. I am grateful for this journey. Feeling my deeper feelings and emotions make me deeper.

My inner pains are part of my beauty. I honor my inner beauty. By honoring my inner beauty, I honor myself. Facing my fears helps me release the feelings I carry. I am soft, sacred energy. My vulnerability is my strength. My transparency is my shield. I don't understand. I will trust in God's heavenly plan. I am grateful for this journey. Everything is always working out for me. If I don't face my fears, then I'll never heal. Everything will be alright. I am not ashamed of who I am. I am healing. I trust in God's plan. I am grateful for this journey. I am authentic.

– TRUST

How do I take care of me?

What am I here to learn? All I have is how I feel. I don't understand. I don't need to understand. I need to trust myself and trust my feelings. Everything is always working out for me. I am here for me. I show up for me. I forgive myself. What is my soul's truth? What am I trying to hide? Negative energy doesn't serve me. Pulling the weeds before they take over is what I know. Being afraid doesn't serve me. Fear drains my energy.

– ACCEPTANCE

What am I here to learn? I am real. I am authentic. Making myself vulnerable is my strength. Staying aligned means allowing. The Holy Spirit fills my heart with love, joy, and abundance. I am filled with positive energy over and over again. Making peace with myself, and accepting where I am, allows me to move forward. My pain and my vulnerability are my strength. I am what I think. I trust that being real with myself is my strength. I love myself. I take care of me. Honesty is my source. I am worthy of everything that comes my way. I am worthy of what I want. What do I desire? I desire love, joy, and abundance. I desire happiness. I am worthy of this happiness. Everything I desire is coming my way because of my loving presence. Everything I desire is magnetically attracted to me. I don't have to be anyone other than me. Every breath I breath fills me with positive energy. Everything I desire is already on its way. I accept who I am. My humility is my strength. I am grateful for everything my heart generates for me in my life. I surrender to my purpose of staying connected to my heart. My transparency is my strength. My heart is love.

– RECEIVE

I trust in God's plan for happiness.

What am I here to learn? I am worthy of everything I desire. I am worthy of receiving abundance. I am open to receiving. I believe in my value. My value is my loving heart. Everything will be okay. Trusting God's plan is my strength. I am magnetic energy. I am full of love and light. I naturally radiate beautiful energy from inside of me. The Holy Spirit regenerates this energy over and over again. Who am I?

What am I here to learn? I am a forgiven child of God. I am feminine energy. Feeling into my pain and confusion gives me strength.

What am I here to learn? I deserve love, joy, and abundance. I am grateful. I trust everything will be okay. I love myself. I take care of me. I take care of my heart. Everything will be okay. Everything I need is deep inside of me.

WEEK 36

– EMPOWERMENT

I believe anything is possible. I embrace surrendering. I embrace God's wisdom. I am energy. My feminine energy is my confidence. My loving presence is my gift. Trusting is my strength. I embody my feminine energy. I am grateful for this journey. I trust in God's heavenly plan. I embrace letting go. I can handle with grace anything that comes my way. I surrender to my purpose of staying connected to my heart.

Everything I desire is being attracted to me. I experience the world through my true feminine center. My true power comes from letting go of control. Getting inside of every moment pulls the world towards me. Everything I desire naturally comes to me. Everything will be okay. I am soft, sacred feminine energy.

– FEEL

What am I here to feel?

What am I here to learn? I am empowered by my feelings. My feminine energy is my power. I am healing and I am growing. My feelings allow me to become the deeper person I am. My feelings are my guide. Everyone deserves happiness. I am dynamic energy. I am who I am. I am authentic. My feelings are a power place. I am not ashamed of my feelings. I know what I feel. I feel with my heart. My feelings make me who I am. My deep feelings make me more of who I am. I honor my feelings. By honoring my feelings, I honor my heart and I honor myself.

– TRUST

Trusting myself is my strength. I am trusting in God's plan. Everything that comes my way helps me connect with myself. I am becoming a deeper person. I am grateful for myself every day. I trust life. I trust everything is always working out for me. I am manifesting everything I desire. Embracing my pain brings me to my higher truth. I am authentic energy. I trust myself. I show up for me. I am committed to me. My commitment to myself makes me feel confident. I resolve to commit to me. As I focus on my inside, the outside world is a byproduct. I love myself and I have compassion on myself. I am infinite potential. All of life's possibilities are being attracted to me. I am anchored in myself. Everything is always working out for me. I am here to trust the process. I deserve positive energy. I deserve deep love, deep joy, and deep abundance. Staying calm grounds me. Staying calm fills my energy and fuels me by the Holy Spirit. As I bring my awareness inward, it makes me more confident. My stillness is my feminine energy. I choose to step into sacred energy. I choose to fill myself with positive energy. I am creating transformation and change in my life. My masculine energy is my shield. I am grateful for this journey. There is no limit to gratitude. I am ready to receive from the universe. I am soft, sacred energy. I honor myself. I honor me.

What am I here to learn? I am sacred energy. I am divinity. I am radiant. That's the seed that allows me to birth the most beautiful life.

– ACCEPTANCE

What am I here to learn? Trusting brings my dream life. Everything I want to attract comes because I trust. My greatest power comes when I receive from the Holy Spirit. I trust in God's heavenly plan for my happiness. God has a better plan for me than I can ever imagine. My pain makes me a deeper person. Abundance is finding me. Abundance is being attracted to me. Everything is always working out for me. I trust in God's plan. I am grateful for this journey. Everything is okay. This is an opportunity for me to learn a new lesson. I am a full-fluid dynamic feminine body. I am filled with deep love, deep joy, and abundance. I attract everything I create inside of me. I am radiant. I accept where I am. I am becoming everything I desire. I am the source of everything I want. I am everything that I think. I am grateful for this journey. I am soft, sacred feminine energy. I have an abundance mindset. I am the creator of everything I desire. I am worthy of everything I desire. My vulnerability is my shield. I am authentic. I am worthy of everything I want. And if I need to face every fear to get there, I will. Life is not scary. I am meant to thrive. Being afraid doesn't serve me. Avoiding pain doesn't serve me. I am grateful for this journey. I am soft, sacred feminine energy.

– RECEIVE

I manifest everything I desire. What do I desire? I surrender to God's plan. I am soft, sacred goddess energy. What energy am I called to create? Abundance flows to me easily and effortlessly every single day. I am grateful for this journey. I am stepping into my full potential. What am I feeling that my soul is drawn to? How do I want to show up? What frequency am I choosing to anchor myself in? I am so grateful for this journey. I am ready to receive abundance. I surrender to God's plan. I am connecting to my sacred energy. I am worthy of receiving everything I desire. I am magnetic energy. I am the holder of beautiful valuable energy. My energy is my value. I am a receiver of good energy. I am worthy of everything I desire because of who I am. I am a receiver of good energy.

My true power is being fully present in every moment. I am valuable energy. I believe in my value. I am a loving heart with a wise soul. I am anchored in my truth. I see myself as a beautiful person. I am worthy of deep joy, deep love, and deep abundance. Amazing things are happening in my life. I deserve good things. I am worthy of manifesting deep abundance. I am open to receiving from life.

What am I here to learn? Everything I desire comes from inside of me. I am a strong, sacred, elevated energy. I attract only energy that makes me feel good and makes me happy. I protect my heart. Only I can heal my heart. I make myself strong and give myself strength. I am worthy of abundance. I am grateful for this journey. I am grateful for finding me.

WEEK 37

– EMPOWERMENT

I am grateful. My energy is my power. My body is magnetic energy. Staying connected to my physical body attracts everything I need in my life. My empowered life comes from inside of me. What am I here to learn? What if I focus on what's not mine? What I'm feeling doesn't match my core energy. Standing up for what I believe is my core. I show up for me. My feminine energy is my strength. I am grounded in everything I believe. Feeling my energy attracts others to me. Trusting is my strength. Experiencing every moment keeps me in my feminine energy.

– FEEL

What am I feeling? I have joy in my heart. Getting in touch with my feelings is my power. I am learning. I am healing. There is a purpose for this journey. Pushing my feelings away does not serve me. My energy makes me stronger. I trust in God's heavenly plan for happiness. My heart is open. I am open to receiving what God is teaching me. I am not afraid of my feelings. I am soft, sacred feminine energy. I am not afraid to be authentic. I only attract energy that matches mine. My feelings are coming from a place of power and not of shame. My emotions are my magnetic energy. What emotions am I feeling in my body? What is my body trying to tell me? My deeper feelings heal me. I only attract positive energy. I am love. I am loving. I am loved. I honor myself. I am growing. I am healing.

– TRUST

Where am I not trusting myself? I trust God and God's plan. I know I can handle any situation that comes my way. My past is not my future. Whatever comes my way I can trust myself. What fits my highest power? I am trustworthy. I trust everything is always working out for me. Every opportunity I have is helping me step up to my higher truth. I learn from every moment. My heart is open. I am worthy of good experiences. I am worthy of abundance. I take care of my inner child. My beauty comes from my heart. My loving presence is my gift to others. I am grateful for this journey. I am manifesting everything I desire. My heart is full. The Holy Spirit regenerates love, joy, and abundance in my heart over and over again. I'm scared. I don't need to understand. I finally know where I belong.

– ACCEPTANCE

I am soft, sacred feminine energy. Everything I've always desired is coming my way. I don't understand. I don't need to understand. I surrender to my heart. I've been given a gift. Life is a gift. I am grateful for this journey. I am here for me. I take care of myself first. I show up for me. Everything is coming together exactly the way it's supposed to. Everything is okay. God has a plan for me that I trust for heavenly happiness. I attract only positive energy. I am grateful. I am at peace with where I am. I am attracting everything I desire. I am attracting deep joy, deep love, and deep happiness. My fear doesn't serve me. I am worth everything that comes my way. Everything that comes my way is what has been planned for me.

– RECEIVE

What is my truth?

What am I here to learn? I am here to heal my heart. I honor my pain. I own my pain. I am patient. I am compassionate with myself. I don't need approval from others. I approve of myself. My power comes from my inner self. I love myself. I am connected to me. I connect to me. I honor me. I surrender to my purpose of staying connected to my heart. My value comes from inside of my heart. I am worthy of abundance. I am worthy of everything I desire. I am valuable energy. I love me. I love myself. My feminine energy is magnetic. I am very valuable. I'm struggling. I am a good receiver. I don't need to prove myself to anyone. I am worthy. I am enough. I can't climb out of this hole. How can I be a better receiver? I am grateful for my value. I trust in God's heavenly plan. I am a beautiful person. I am worthy of abundance. I surrender to my purpose of staying connected to my heart. How do I become a better receiver? I need to accept where I am and be at peace.

WEEK 38

– EMPOWERMENT

I am here because I am committed to me. I don't need to prove myself to anyone. I am happy. I am full of joy. My heart is always open. I deserve respect. I deserve abundance. Why am I intimidated by everyone? Why am I paranoid? Why do I doubt myself? I trust God's heavenly plan. I am a forgiven child of God. I am a better person. I am grateful. I can learn from this. I know how I feel. I want to be comfortable and confident being me.

My empowered world comes from my physical energy. My goal today is to slow down every moment so that I feel the ease and the grace I deserve. I don't like who I am when I'm afraid. I don't like being around negativity. My loving presence is my greatest gift. My truth is my feminine energy. My confidence comes from my heart. I am fully present with myself. I am not here to impress anyone. I have a gift of showing love to others. That gift is from the Holy Spirit who shines in me every day, every hour, every minute, every second. My spirit is beautiful and caring. I will trust this feeling and embrace every moment. I trust in God's heavenly plan. I am strong.

My focus is my business and my family. Only I can make myself happy. My growth has to come from trusting myself. Every sign I see is a mirror that I am attracting abundance. This is where my heart belongs.

– FEEL

My feelings are so confused. My pain makes me stronger. I am learning to trust. My heart hurts. Everything I need to make me happy comes from inside of me. What am I feeling? I'm feeling love throughout my body. Everything will be okay. I will be okay. God has a plan for me. I surrender to my purpose of staying connected to my heart. I am dynamic. I am full of love. I love myself. I love my inner child. My beauty is my feminine energy. I honor my beauty. I am worthy of deep respect and deep abundance. My confidence and my beauty come from my feminine energy. I am worthy of abundance. Everything I desire I am manifesting. I am worthy of everything I desire.

– TRUST

What am I here to learn? I am stepping into my power. I trust myself to know everything is always working out for me. There must be value in this. I trust in God's heavenly plan for happiness. The Holy Spirit fills my soul and regenerates love inside of me over and over again. Everything is always working out for me. I surrender to my purpose of staying connected to my heart.

What am I here to learn? Where am I not trusting myself? I attract only high-level energy. Why do I worry? I am committed to me. Abundance flows to me easily and effortlessly every single day. I am manifesting everything I need. My heart is open. My masculine energy disciplines me. I hurt. I can embrace the pain. I'm tired of this journey. It hurts entirely too much. I don't like the pain, and I don't understand. I don't need to understand. I don't want to open myself up anymore, but this the only way to make me stronger. I love myself. I honor myself. I am soft, sacred energy. How does walking away from the pain serve me? The pain makes me angry. The pain makes me sad. Feeling the pain makes me stronger. I deserve abundance. I take care of me. I'm the only one who can love me the way I desire. Everything will be okay. I trust my heart. I surrender to my purpose of staying connected to my heart. I deserve better.

– ACCEPTANCE

I am manifesting good things. Good things are being attracted to me. The Holy Spirit fills me with deep love, deep joy, and deep abundance. I am attracting everything I desire. I don't understand. I don't need to understand. I trust in God's plan. Everything is always working out for me. Things are working the way they are supposed to. I am learning a new lesson. This is an opportunity for my own well-being. I am a full-fluid dynamic energy. I only attract positive energy. I am what I think. I am the creator of everything I desire. Everything will be okay. I am soft, sacred feminine energy. I am worthy of everything I desire. I am not in control. I am excited to be living an abundant life. I am attracting everything I desire because of who I am. I am not afraid of being me. I trust in God's plan. There is a purpose for this and I will trust everything will be okay. I surrender to my loving heart. The more time I spend with my heart and getting to know my feelings, the stronger and more confident I become. I have compassion on me. Every feeling is as important as the next. My discomfort empowers me. I deserve happiness. If I desire it, I deserve it. I am willing to learn from my pain. I embrace myself and all my wounds. I am anchored in me. I show up for me.

– RECEIVE

Who am I? I am somebody. I am me. My confidence comes from my heart. My purpose is staying connected to my heart. I have compassion for me. Everything will be okay. I live from my core energy. My external world is a reflection of my internal world. I am grateful for this journey. I am becoming a better me. I deserve abundance. I attract abundance. I am above all the pain in this world. I am amazing energy. I am ready to receive abundance. My value and my worth are my energy. I am worthy of everything I desire. I don't have to *do* anything to be valuable. My heart is magnetic energy. I am a receiver of good energy. My heart is full of joy. I am valuable energy. I believe in my value. I am a loving heart. I see myself as a loving heart. I see myself as a beautiful person. I am worthy of high-level energy. I am worthy of receiving abundance. Everything I desire I am worthy of receiving. I am open to receive deep energy from the Holy Spirit.

WEEK 39

– EMPOWERMENT

I am committed to me. I am attracting abundance. I am here to take care of myself and my heart. I am grateful for who I am. I am grateful for finding myself. I am grateful for this EMPOWERMENT. I am okay. Being overwhelmed doesn't serve me. I honor myself. I make myself happy. My business fills my heart with joy. I am making amazing progress. I am taking massive action. What I have learned has made me incredibly strong and confident. I am blessed. The Holy Spirit is in me.

– FEEL

I learn more about me when I dig deeper inside of me. I am my own hero. I make myself feel good. My strength comes from inside my heart. I love myself. Suppressing my feelings doesn't serve me. My feelings make me stronger and deeper. My feelings are my best friends. I trust in God's heavenly plan for happiness. My heart is open. I am my best friend. I don't ignore myself. I love myself. I am authentic. I attract only positive energy. I am magnetic energy and I am attracting abundance. My inner child is hurt, but I'm strong. I am here for me. I show up for me. I am grateful for this journey. I am not attached to anyone. I am healing. I am building abundance in my life. Everything will be okay. I am worthy of everything I desire. I am an elevated woman. I honor myself. I honor my feelings. I am worthy of everything I desire. I am a forgiven child of God. Jesus holds my hand. I am worthy of everything I desire. I am ready to receive abundance. I am excited to be building abundance. I am grateful to find me. I am my own confidence.

– TRUST

My happiness comes from inside of me. I deserve honor. I deserve respect. I choose courage over fear. I have compassion on me. I step into my power of my feminine energy. What is my true core? I deserve love and honor.

What am I here to learn? I take care of myself. I surrender to my purpose of staying connected to my heart. I am grateful for this journey. I am anchored in my breath. How do I protect myself? I don't need to protect myself. I don't need to avoid pain because I know I have strength in my pain. I trust in God's plan for happiness. I am soft, sacred, fluid energy. The Holy Spirit lifts me up. My true happiness comes from my internal world. Trusting is my strength. My only plan is to take care of me. I trust in God's plan, and I will hold Jesus' hand every step of the way. I am full of love. I am free to be me.

– ACCEPTANCE

I am worthy of high-level energy. I feel good. I am attracting abundance. I am a receiver of good energy. I am soft, sacred feminine energy. The universe takes care of me. The Holy Spirit fills me with positive energy. I show up for me. Everything is okay. This is an opportunity for me to learn a new lesson. I am regenerating energy and fullness over and over again. What am I creating? I am fullness. I accept where I am. I am the creator of everything I desire. Feeling my heart is my strength. I am worthy of everything that comes my way.

– RECEIVE

I am worthy of everything I desire. I am a high-value woman. I feel my value. I deserve positive energy. I am worthy of everything I desire. I receive only good energy. I am the holder of beautiful valuable energy. I am worthy just because of who I am. Happiness comes from trusting. I trust in God's heavenly plan. I am a receiver of good energy. I am valuable energy. I believe in my value. I am anchored in my truth. I am a beautiful person. I surrender to my purpose. My purpose is my loving heart. The Holy Spirit breathes deep love, deep joy, and deep abundance. I am ready to be a receiver. I trust in God's plan for happiness. I am grateful for this journey. I am magnetic feminine energy. My loving presence is my gift to others. I radiate fullness. Everything is okay. Everything will be okay.

WEEK 40

– EMPOWERMENT

I am committed to me. I'm feeling stuck. I'm trying to be at peace, but I'm torn. I'm over- analyzing. I'm afraid. I'm disappointed. I'm confused. I know what I need to do. My power comes from my heart. I'm scared though. My brain is spinning. I am empowered. I am staying connected to my inner wisdom.

My intention today is noticing when I'm in my head and on autopilot. My focus is my inner energy first and then staying grounded. My morning inner work helps me step into my true physical self. I no longer run on autopilot. I embrace myself. I get inside of every moment which brings the world to me. I am experiencing every moment. My feminine energy attracts others to my magnetic energy. This is my confidence. I am filled with the Holy Spirit and with love.

– FEEL

What am I feeling? I am feeling deep love, deep joy, and deep abundance. I am grateful for this journey. I am excited about life. I can handle anything. I take care of me. I am my strength. Trusting is my power. I surrender to my emotions. I am brave. My fear doesn't serve me. I am finding me. I am authentic energy. I surrender to my purpose of staying connected to my heart. I protect my inner child. My feelings are my power. I am strong. My life is full. I can let go of the pain. How is this pain serving me? What am I getting out of this pain? By honoring my pain, I honor myself. I deserve abundance. I am filled with the Holy Spirit. I am filled with amazing energy. I make myself feel good. I am authentic soft, sacred feminine energy.

– TRUST

I am light. I am love. I forgive myself. I am grateful for finding me. I am finding financial abundance. I deserve this energy. I honor my boundaries. I surrender to not knowing the answers. I am a deep, caring, and loving energy. I am soft and sacred. Everything will be okay. Everything is okay. I trust in God's heavenly plan. I will be okay. Abundance flows to me easily and effortlessly every single day. The seeds for deep joy, deep happiness, and deep abundance have been planted. I am grateful for this journey.

I surrender to my purpose of staying connected to my heart. I am spontaneous. I am letting go of control. Things seem to work out better than I can imagine. How am I not trusting others? I am trusting the universe will bring things together. I trust I can handle any situation. I am learning from this pain. My value as a woman comes from trusting God. I am becoming a deeper soul. I am grateful for being me. My true power comes from my feminine energy. Trusting is so hard. There must be value in this. What am I here to learn?

Trusting my intuition and my boundaries make me feel good. I surrender to my purpose of staying connected to my heart. I trust everything will be okay. I am grateful for this journey. I forgive myself. I can trust myself by staying committed to myself. I love myself. I love my inner child. I am committed to my inner child. I am staying committed to my healing. I am worthy of deep love, deep happiness, and deep abundance. Only I can make myself feel safe and secure. I am love. I am loving. I am loved.

– ACCEPTANCE

God has a plan. Trusting is my strength. I surrender to God's plan. Everything is okay, and this is an opportunity for me to grow. I am a full, dynamic woman regenerating energy over and over again. What am I attracting? I accept where and who I am. I am magnetic positive energy. Everything I desire is being attracted to me. My heart hurts. Everything will be okay. Being scared and afraid doesn't serve me. My heart hurts. I have to be strong. I become stronger and stronger every day. I am here to make me happy. I have no regrets. I am always learning. I am grateful for this journey. My vulnerability and transparency are my shield. Jesus holds my hand and gives me strength.

– RECEIVE

I receive good energy. My value is my energy. I am grateful for this journey. I am valuable energy. I am worthy of everything I desire. I am magnetic energy. I am the holder of beautiful valuable energy. I am receiving everything I desire. My empowered life is coming to me because of who I am. My heart is open. I am a receiver of good energy. My core power comes from within. I am anchored in my truth. My truth is I am a beautiful person. My confidence comes from my heart. I surrender to my purpose of staying connected to my heart. I am worthy of everything I desire because of who I am. I am grateful for this journey. I surrender to my vulnerability. I surrender to my purpose of staying connected to my heart. My transparency is my shield.

WEEK 41

– EMPOWERMENT

I am committed to me and being more of who I really am. I am learning to embody my femininity. My power comes from when I drop into my heart. I am anchored in my body. I am magnetic energy. I feel my confidence. I am connected to my physical self. I deserve abundance. I am attracting abundance. My self-confidence is building because of what energy I feel in my body. I am graceful. I am radiant. The Holy Spirit fills me with love, joy, and happiness. I trust in God's heavenly plan for pure joy, peace, and happiness.

I am enjoying the journey. Everything is working out the way it's supposed to be. Everything comes to me with ease and grace. I am grateful for this journey. I am gentle. I am soft. I am healing. Breathing helps me ground my inner energy. The source of my true power is inside of me. I always have the option of connecting to myself—and this is my greatest gift as a woman. I am a gift. I deserve to be cherished. This is my truth.

– FEEL

I am feminine energy. Feeling my emotions make me a deeper energy. Getting in touch with my feelings empowers me as a full person. My feminine energy is connected to my feelings. Avoiding my feelings doesn't serve me. I become stronger in myself as I feel all my emotions. My feelings are my guide. Trusting is how I find my confidence. Understanding my emotions and feelings amplifies me as a woman. I am authentic energy. I am not afraid to be me. I attract only positive energy. I surrender to my purpose of staying connected to my heart. I have discovered how to feel safe and secure again. All my confidence comes from trusting. I will be okay. I love myself. What am I here to learn? I have boundaries and I honor myself. I am a high-value woman and deserve everything I desire. Abundance flows to me easily and effortlessly every single day.

I am not afraid to walk away from the pain. I am beautiful soft, sacred energy. I am grateful for this journey. Surrender makes me more loving. Letting go of the negative makes me more magnetic. I can do anything I put my mind to. Letting go of negative feelings makes me stronger. No more fear. No more guilt. I am positive. I have positive feelings and thoughts. I embrace staying positive.

– TRUST

I show up for me because that's all I have. I'm grateful for a journal that brings me closer to finding my purpose and that allows me to find myself. I am grateful for finding myself. I am soft, sacred feminine energy. My feminine energy is my confidence. It doesn't matter what anyone else says or thinks about me. My energy is what gives me value. The energy I hold is what attracts others to me. Trusting is what gives me happiness. Trusting is my confidence. I am energy. I am sacred power. I am filled up on the inside. I am connected to myself. The energy inside of me is my power. I trust in God's plan for happiness. My worth is not from others. I am building my dream life and I am becoming stronger. I deserve respect.

Everything is always working out for me. There must be value in this. I am the only person who can show up for me. I'm supposed to trust. I don't understand. I don't need to understand. I am committed to me. I am grateful for this journey, but my heart hurts. My faith is my reason. My faith is my focus. The seeds have been manifested and planted. My happiness comes from trusting everything will be okay, and that God has a beautiful plan for me. I am ready to receive God's abundance.

– ACCEPTANCE

Why am I here? What are my core values? I trust in God's plan for happiness. Everything will be okay. I attract only positive energy. I don't attract pain. My purpose in life is staying connected to my heart. I make myself happy. I choose happiness. I only attract abundance. Allowing the Holy Spirit, and not trying to control an outcome, gives me peace. I am a full-fluid dynamic energy. The Holy Spirit regenerates fullness and abundance into my life. I am at peace with where I am. Abundance flows to me easily and effortlessly every day. My heart is love. Feeling my pain is my strength. What is my pain? What am I feeling?

What am I here to learn? I don't understand. I don't need to understand. I want to walk away from the pain. I want to be stronger. I want more confidence. I have so many thoughts, and I don't understand any of them. Feeling my pain makes me stronger. Feeling my pain gives me more confidence. My heart is healing. My life is full, and I am grateful. I am grateful for this journey, and for learning to think differently.

– RECEIVE

Receiving is feminine energy. I am valuable energy just because of who I am. I am open to receiving positive energy. I am a good receiver. I believe in my value. I am beautiful energy. My true power comes from how I feel on the inside. I am worthy of everything I desire. I am manifesting abundance in my life. I am the center of everything I desire.

WEEK 42

– EMPOWERMENT

What am I here to learn? I am becoming more of who I am. My energy is soft, sacred feminine energy. My power and energy are what I feel in my physical body. My power comes from trusting. The solutions I need don't come from my mind. My magnetic energy attracts everything I need in life. I am connected to my true inner wisdom. I am pulling the whole world towards me.

Every day I find ways to get inside my body. My empowered life comes from connecting with myself. I surrender to my true power. I experience the world from my true feminine center. I am grateful for this journey and completely understand I can embrace the journey and dynamic feelings.

My purpose is staying connected to my heart. I find peace in experiencing every moment. The sensations I feel make me feel more feminine. By focusing on ease and grace embodies my feminine energy.

I show up for me. I am worthy of abundance. I am trustworthy. I am love and kindness. *My loving presence is my greatest gift.*

– FEEL

What is my energy? What energy do I want to be? My energy is magnetic energy. My heart is open. I am attracting abundance. I am centered in my body. Everything I desire I manifest naturally. I am dynamic energy. My true power comes from surrendering to my purpose. My purpose is staying connected to my heart.

What am I here to learn? What questions do I need to ask? I am energy. I am sacred power. I am soft and sacred. The Holy Spirit fills me with divine energy. I am connected to myself, and that is my power. My feelings are empowering. What I feel is my power. I am growing. I am becoming deeper as I experience my pain. I am grateful for this journey. Living in my head doesn't serve me. I know my core is magnetic. I am afraid of being bold. Why am I suppressing my emotions? Why am I afraid to speak from my heart? What am I embarrassed about?

I am feminine energy. I am soft and sacred. My masculine energy protects me. I am rooted in my core energy. My core energy is my magnetic power. I honor the goddess deep inside of me. I honor myself. I protect my inner child. I surrender to my core. My core is my loving heart. I trust my core energy. My core is my magnetic energy. I trust myself. I believe in myself. I trust my core energy. The Holy Spirit fills my heart with deep love, deep happiness, and deep abundance.

– TRUST

I am committed to myself and to my dream life. I am grateful. I surrender to whatever this is. I know that God has a heavenly plan—and I can't force anything. I trust in God's heavenly plan for true happiness and joy. I'm where I'm meant to be. I trust in God's plan and that I don't need to do anything to push things along. I am worthy. I am deserving. I am anchored inside of me. I am stepping into my power. I trust myself to "respond only" when feeling fear instead of judging or taking action. I don't need to solve every problem. I know that everything is always working out for me. My strength is my healing. I can wait. I am healing. My power is to respond. I have to trust that this is my true power. I'm allowing. I am committed to me. I'm committed to protecting me and my inner child. I am my own strength. I have compassion for me when I feel alone. I will trust God's plan. I want to be me. My confidence comes from my heart and the Holy Spirit fills me up.

— ACCEPTANCE

Trusting allows the dream life I desire. Everything I desire is waiting for me. My greatest power comes from receiving the Holy Spirit. Trusting God's plan gives me peace. Abundance is being attracted to me. Everything is always working out for me. Everything is falling together the way it's supposed to. The seed has been planted for me to gain my self-confidence. The Holy Spirit regenerates energy over and over again inside of me. I am full of love. I am attracting everything that matches how I feel inside of me. Making peace with my energy makes me feel good. I am the source of everything I want. I am what I think, and my life is a result of this. I love myself. I take care of me. I protect my inner child. I am the creator of everything I desire. The Holy Spirit inspires me. I am magnetic energy. Everything I desire is attracted to me.

— RECEIVE

I am worthy of receiving everything I desire. My gift to others is my loving presence. I am magnetic energy. My energy is my value. I surrender to God's plan. I am worthy of abundance. I am grateful for this journey. I am happier than I have ever been in my entire life. I am a receiver of good energy. I am a high-value woman. I believe in my core. I am anchored in my feminine energy. I am worthy of high-level energy. I am worthy of abundance. I am worthy of receiving abundance. I am grateful for this journey. I show up for me every day. Abundance shows up for me every day. I am open to receiving everything I desire.

WEEK 43

– EMPOWERMENT

What am I feeling? Staying in my body is my strength. I am anchored in my core. What am I here to learn? I don't understand. My feminine energy is my confidence. I am grateful for this journey. I don't understand. I don't need to understand. I am grateful for this journey. I show up for myself. I am anchored in my feminine energy. I am attracting everything I need in my life. I am soft, sacred feminine energy.

I am manifesting abundance. My empowered life comes from what I feel inside of me. My loving presence is my gift to others. The Holy Spirit fills me with deep love, deep joy, and deep abundance. I embrace every single moment. I am worthy of abundance. I am love.

– FEEL

What am I here to learn? I am courage. I am divine energy. I am worthy of abundance. I am smart. I am dynamic. I am soft, sacred energy. My feminine energy is empowered energy. I am full-embodied energy. I am vibrant. I attract only positive energy. I am worthy of everything I desire. I am open to receiving abundance. My heart is open. I am authentic energy. I am who I am. I deserve abundance. I am empowered energy. My deeper feelings make me stronger. I only attract high-level energy. What am I feeling? I am okay. Everything will be okay. I am divine energy. The Holy Spirit fills me up over and over again with deep love, deep joy, and deep abundance. I am an elevated woman filled with goddess energy. I surrender to my purpose of staying connected to my heart. I am grateful for this journey. My confidence comes from my heart. My inner strength is my beauty. I honor my heart. By honoring my heart, I honor my beauty.

– TRUST

I surrender. I surrender to my thoughts. I trust in God's heavenly plan. I am an elevated woman with high value. I am worthy of abundance. Trusting is my strength. Everything will be okay. Everything is always working out for me. I have an abundance mindset. I am worthy of everything I desire. I am grateful for this journey. I'm scared. Being afraid doesn't serve me.

– ACCEPTANCE

I allow only positive energy to be attracted to me. I am grateful for this journey. Everything will be okay. I feel good. I am aligned with my core values. I trust in God's plan for heavenly happiness. I am not in control. God's plan is better than any that I can create. Abundance is being attracted to me. Everything I am experiencing is happening the way it's supposed to. Everything is okay. This is an opportunity for me to grow. My energy is full. The Holy Spirit regenerates life in me over and over again. I am attracting abundance. I am the source of everything I want. My greatest power is getting real with myself so I can embody the positive energy I deserve. I regenerate positive energy within me. I am everything I desire. I am worthy of everything that comes my way. What I want, I am worthy. I am grateful for everything my heart generates for me. I honor my heart. I surrender to my heart.

– RECEIVE

I am a receiver of good energy. My worthiness lies in my energy. I am magnetic energy. I am anchored in the truth. I am grateful for this journey. I am valuable energy. The Holy Spirit fills me with the energy I need. Jesus holds my hand. Staying grounded and staying in my feminine energy is my strength. I surrender to my purpose of staying connected to my heart. I am soft, sacred feminine energy. I am a forgiven child of God.

What am I here to learn? My heart is magnetic energy. I am a receiver of good energy. I am soft, sacred feminine energy. I don't need to do anything to prove my value to anyone.

WEEK 44

– EMPOWERMENT

My power comes from my heart. Overthinking doesn't serve me. I trust myself. I show up for myself. With grace I can handle anything that comes my way. Staying connected to my body draws everything to me. I am grounded in my energy. My empowered feminine energy comes from my heart. I am grounded in my soft, sacred energy. I am worthy of elevated energy. I surrender to God's plan for heavenly happiness. I am healing. I am becoming stronger. I don't always have to understand. I'm tired of being afraid. My loving presence is my greatest power as a woman.

– FEEL

What am I feeling? I am authentic. My feelings come from a place of power, not a place of shame. I am soft, sacred energy. I am manifesting everything I desire. I surrender to my purpose of staying connected to my heart. Only I can take care of myself. I am here to take care of me. I am love. I am full of love. My heart is full of abundance. My pain gives me depth. My feelings are my best friends. My heart is open. I am becoming a deeper me. I am dynamic feminine energy. My feelings are my place of power. I surrender to my purpose of staying connected to my heart. My confidence comes from my heart. My confidence comes from my soft, sacred feminine energy. What am I feeling? I am feeling fear. What am I afraid of? I'm afraid of change. I'm afraid I could be wrong. I'm afraid I will make a mistake. Everything is always working out for me. I trust in God's heavenly plan for happiness. I will be okay. Everything will be okay. Everything is always working out for me.

What am I here to learn? Trusting is my strength. Trusting God's plan is my strength. My fear is my strength. My fear makes me a deeper person. My feminine energy is magnetic. I am attracting abundance into my life.

– TRUST

I am trustworthy. I trust in God's heavenly plan for happiness. I am grateful for this journey. Everything is okay. Everything will be okay. I am becoming a deeper soul. I'm afraid. Fear means growth. My energy is my true power. I trust my intuition and my boundaries. I attract only positive energy. Everything is always working out for me. I am healing. Feeling my pain makes me stronger. I attract only high-level relationships. I am committed to me. I take care of me. I show up for me. I deserve abundance. Showing up for me makes me feel good. I have only love in my heart. My loving presence is my gift to others. My gentleness and vulnerability are my shield. The Holy Spirit fills my heart with deep love, deep joy, and deep abundance. This is my truth. My inner feels are my strength. I value myself. I honor my soul. I cherish myself.

– ACCEPTANCE

Allowing is my strength. My life has always been pain. The Holy Spirit fills me up and regenerates love, joy, and abundance inside of me over and over again. I trust in God's heavenly plan. Trusting is my strength. My strength comes from my feminine energy. Everything is working out the way it's supposed to. I am full energy. I am creating abundance in my life. I am grateful for this journey. I am becoming what I believe. I am what I think, and my life is a result of this. My heart is open, and I am attracting everything I desire.

– RECEIVE

I am a receiver of good energy. The Holy Spirit fills me up over and over again. I am grateful for this journey. I am soft, sacred feminine energy. My transparency is my shield. I am worthy of receiving abundance. I show up for me. Abundance shows up for me. I honor myself. I honor my feminine energy. I attract everything I feel inside of me. I am love. I am loving. I am loved. I am worthy of good friendships. The Holy Spirit fills me up. Jesus holds my hand. I trust in God's heavenly plan.

WEEK 45

– EMPOWERMENT

What am I feeling? I am experiencing confusion. I want someone to tell me what to do. I am tired. My body is tired. I am in control. I am entered in my heart. I am grateful for this journey. I can handle with grace anything that comes my way. My magnetic force is my confidence. Staying connected to my physical body attracts everything I desire. My true power lies inside of my heart. I am grounded in my feminine energy. I acknowledge my empowered life comes from inside my heart. I am soft, sacred feminine energy. All of my feelings are worthy of experiencing. Everything I desire naturally comes to me with ease and grace.

– FEEL

My feelings are my intuition. Trusting is my strength. I am worthy of joy and abundance. I trust that God has a plan. I will be okay. Everything is always working out for me. Feeling these deep feelings make me stronger. No one gets to treat me poorly. I have boundaries. I love myself. I honor myself. My magnetic energy attracts everything I desire. I desire abundance. I am worthy of abundance. The Holy Spirit fills my heart with beautiful energy. My energy is my beauty. I am grateful for finding myself. I will find the words. I am trustworthy. My deepest pain is my strength. I know the truth. I need to take care of me and honor my inner goddess. I am a goddess inside, and I deserve respect. Everything will be okay. Everything I need is coming my way. I am worthy of everything I desire.

– TRUST

I show up for me. I am trustworthy and abundance shows up for me. I trust in God's heavenly plan. My energy is amazing. I am stepping into my power. I trust that everything is always working out for me. I surrender to my vulnerability. I am soft, sacred feminine energy. Everything is always working out for me. I am committed to myself. I honor me. I am my top priority. I desire deep love, deep joy, and deep abundance.

I am worthy of everything I desire. I surrender to trusting. My beauty is my energy. I radiate beauty. The Holy Spirit radiates amazing energy inside of me. I am a light that attracts others.

– ACCEPTANCE

I am grateful. Trusting is my strength. My feminine energy is my confidence. I am always receiving good energy. I am worthy of abundance and deep joy. I trust in God's plan for happiness. I am attracting everything I desire. I am worthy of everything my heart desires. I am grateful for this journey. Everything will be okay. I trust in God's plan.

– RECEIVE

I am a receiver of good energy. Trusting is my strength. My worthiness is anchored in my energy. I am the holder of beautiful and valuable energy. I surrender to my purpose of staying connected to my heart. I am worthy. I am valuable. My core value comes from my loving nature. I am a receiver of good energy. I am worthy of abundance. I am grateful for this journey.

WEEK 46

– EMPOWERMENT

I am experiencing confusion. I have compassion on my confusion. Confusion is an emotion I am experiencing. I am becoming more of who I am by staying connected to my body. I am soft, sacred feminine energy. My power comes from my purpose. My purpose is staying connected to my heart. I don't have a solution. I don't understand. I trust myself and I show up for myself. I am grounded in my physical self. I am connected to me. I am empowered because of my peace. My energy is my priority. My empowered life comes from how I feel in my heart.

– FEEL

I am attracting everything I desire. I am manifesting abundance. My feelings make me deeper. My feelings are my guide. My heart is open. What am I feeling? What am I here to learn? I only attract good energy. Staying connected to my heart is my purpose. Who am I? I am soft, sacred feminine energy. My feelings are my confidence. I am becoming more comfortable at expressing and experiencing feeling these deeper feelings. By honoring my heart, I honor myself. I am grateful for this journey.

– TRUST

I am trustworthy. I am a leader. People are watching me. I am a good person. I attract positive energy. I am magnetic energy. I am worthy of everything I desire. Abundance is attracted to me. The Holy Spirit fills me with abundance and regenerates deep love, deep joy, and deep abundance inside of me over and over again. I take care of me. I take care of my inner child. Everything will be okay.

– ACCEPTANCE

God has a plan. I am soft, sacred energy. Trusting is my strength. I am aligned in my feminine energy. I am the receiver of deep love, deep joy, and deep abundance in my heart. My vulnerability and transparency are my strength. I am manifesting everything I desire. Everything is going to be okay. Everything is coming together the way it's supposed to. This is an opportunity for me to learn this new lesson. I am a full, fluid and dynamic gorgeous body regenerating over and over and over again. I am worthy of abundance. Trusting is my strength. I accept who I am. I am beautiful feminine energy.

– RECEIVE

I am a high-value woman. I believe in my core value. My worth comes from inside my heart. I surrender to my purpose of staying connected to my heart. I am strong, confident energy. My gift to others is my loving presence. I am the holder of beautiful, valuable energy. I am soft, sacred, and beautiful. I am the receiver of good energy.

What am I here to learn? I am fully present in every moment. My heart is full of joy. The Holy Spirit fills my heart deeply over and over again. I am a high-value woman. I believe in my core values. I am anchored by my truth. I am a beautiful woman. I am grateful for this journey, and I am worthy of everything I desire. I receive only good energy. I am a leader. I am worthy of leadership energy. I show up for myself. Abundance shows up for me. My heart is healing. I forgive myself. I am a forgiven child of God. I deserve abundance. I listen to myself. I enjoy the quiet. My purpose is staying connected to my heart. I am the receiver of good energy. My loving presence is my gift to others.

WEEK 47

– EMPOWERMENT

I am becoming more of who I am. Staying in my energy and in my body are my strength. My body and my heart create a magnetic field. Staying connected to my physical body allows me to attract everything I need. Problem solving comes naturally to me. Staying connected to my heart requires effort. Staying connected to my heart pulls the whole world to me. Staying grounded in myself allows me to be more confident. Staying centered in my energy keeps me soft and sacred. Staying still and closing my eyes helps me stay centered.

Spending time with myself physically every day keeps my body moving. Physically moving my body helps me get out of my head. Staying focused in the moment helps me experience every emotion. Feeling my emotions and experiencing pain and joy is the definition of feminine energy. By embracing these emotions, I am becoming stronger and more confident. Avoiding emotions doesn't serve me. Gratitude allows me to feel my emotions. Confusion is an emotion just like guilt, shame, and jealousy. If I don't allow myself to feel these strong emotions, I will never find confidence. Listening to my heart is my deepest emotion. Visiting these emotions builds my character. My purpose is staying connected to my heart.

— FEEL

What am I feeling? What's in my heart?

What am I here to learn? My core power is my strength. My feelings are my guide. I am grateful for this journey. Trusting is my strength. I surrender to my purpose of staying connected to my heart. I am healing. My pain makes me stronger and deeper. I am grounded in my feminine energy. The Holy Spirit regenerates feminine energy in me. I honor the inner goddess inside me. All my emotions make me stronger. Feeling hurt, frustration, embarrassment, and disappointment are all emotions that are important to feel. My core power is my strength. My core values are my faith, family, and health. My authenticity makes me stronger. I show up for myself. Abundance shows up for me. I am magnetic energy. Everything will be okay. I am grateful for this journey. My loving presence is my gift.

— TRUST

I trust God's heavenly plan for happiness. Everything is always working out for me. Everyone deserves happiness. My pain is my strength. I am grateful for this journey. I am committed to myself. I show up for myself every single day. Abundance shows up for me. Abundance flows to me easily and effortlessly every single day. I am worthy of abundance. I am trustworthy. I am soft, sacred feminine energy. The Holy Spirit lifts me up. Jesus holds my hand.

— ACCEPTANCE

I am grateful for this journey. By "allowing," it attracts everything I desire. I am worthy of abundance. Taking care of myself and giving myself love is where my strength comes from. I am not in control. I trust in God's plan for my happiness. Everything is okay. Everything will be okay. I am learning a new lesson. I am regenerating love, joy, and abundance inside of me over and over again. The Holy Spirit fills me up. I am attracting everything I am creating inside of me. I accept who I am. I am manifesting abundance. I show up for myself every day. Abundance shows up for me every day. I am what I think. I am a magnet. I attract happiness and positive energy. I am the creator of everything I desire. Jesus holds my hand every step of the way. I am grateful for finding myself. I am worthy of everything that comes my way. I am love. I am loving. I am loved.

– RECEIVE

I am worthy of receiving deep joy, deep love, and deep abundance from the Holy Spirit. I regenerate my feminine energy over and over again. I am anchored in my feminine energy. I am soft, sacred feminine energy. I surrender to my purpose of staying connected to my heart. My energy is very valuable. I am a receiver of good energy. I don't need to prove my worthiness to anyone. I am worthy because of who I am. My true power is receiving what I am given. I surrender to my heart. My value comes from inside of me. I am attracting high level energy. I am worthy of abundance. I am worthy of receiving positive energy. I am fullness. I am the receiver of good energy. Everything I desire is coming my way. I am manifesting everything I desire in life. Who am I? I am soft, sacred feminine energy. The Holy Spirit fills me with deep joy, deep love, and deep abundance. My transparency is my shield. Trusting is my strength. I am not an instigator. I am not a manipulator. I am an influencer. I lead with my soft, sacred feminine energy. I trust in God's plan, not mine.

WEEK 48

– EMPOWERMENT

Going through the mountain is more difficult than going around it. Feeling every emotion builds my confidence. My power comes from feeling my emotions. Worry does not serve me. Attracting abundance comes from staying with my feelings. I know I can handle with grace anything that comes my way. I am empowered by trusting and staying connected with my heart. Staying grounded physically pulls the whole world towards me. Tending to my energy is easy to forget, but it is what matters most. Trusting is my strength. What am I here to learn?

Acknowledging my magnetic energy comes when I surrender to my purpose of staying connected to my heart. Slowing down and enjoying every moment allows me to stay in my true power. Getting inside of every moment pulls abundance towards me. This builds my empowered feminine energy. Focusing on my sensations allows everything I desire to flow to me with ease and grace. I am grateful for this journey.

Feeling my vulnerability and transparency allows me to build my confidence. I am anchored to my feelings. What does my body crave naturally? My confidence comes from feeling my heart. My empowered life comes from the inside not the external world. Keeping the energy moving allows me to step into my true power. Experiencing myself in every moment empowers and strengthens me. It feels wonderful to be in touch with my inner energy which is my true power. My heart is connected to my power within me. Enjoying every experience allows me to feel my confidence and my truth.

– FEEL

I am manifesting everything I desire. I am becoming more of me. I am becoming stronger and deeper energy. My heart is open. My emotions make me a deeper soul. I am authentic energy. Everything is going to be okay. I trust God's plan for happiness. I attract only positive energy. I show up for me. Abundance shows up for me. I honor myself. I honor my soft, loving heart. I am a beautiful goddess. I surrender to my purpose of staying connected to my loving heart. I make time for myself every day. I am grateful for this journey. Everything happens for a reason.

– TRUST

What am I here to learn? I surrender to God's plan. I have no plan. I can only trust. My vibration is fear. Fear does not serve me. Transparency is my armor. I show up for me. Everything is always working out for me. Showing up for me builds trust in myself. My true value and worth as a woman come from my purpose. Staying committed to myself builds trust. I am trustworthy. I show up for myself. Abundance shows up for me. I am soft, sacred feminine energy. I am worthy of abundance.

Abundance flows to me easily and effortlessly every single day. I am worthy of abundance. I am learning to be me and love me.

– ACCEPTANCE

Abundance flows to me easily and effortlessly every day. The seed has been planted. I am a loving, caring person. I am a leader. People are following me. I am a higher vibration. I like this vibration. It's a feeling. The vibration is the movement of my heart. I am so grateful for this journey. I believe in myself. I am good enough. I do deserve love, joy, and abundance. Everything will be okay. I am magnetic energy. People are attracted to me. My purpose is staying connected to my heart. My heart is open. I am beautiful. I am beautiful energy.

What am I here to learn? I have no regrets. Regret creates sadness. Regret shows up in ways that we subconsciously choose. I am here to love me and take care of me. I trust in God's plan for happiness. Everything will be okay. I choose happiness. My inspiration comes from the Holy Spirit.

– RECEIVE

I am soft, sacred feminine energy. My value is my positive nature. I show up for me. Abundance shows up for me. My loving presence is my gift to others. I am magnetic energy. I am the holder of beautiful valuable energy. I am a receiver of good energy. The Holy Spirit fills me up and regenerates fullness inside of me over and over again. My heart is open. I am a receiver of good energy. I am valuable energy. I am high-value. My core power comes from within. My loving heart anchors me. I am a beautiful soul. I attract only positive energy. I am worthy of high-level energy. Everything is always working out for me. I am a receiver of good energy. The universe is giving abundance to me. I am forgiveness. I am a forgiven child of God. I am a gracious receiver. Trusting is my strength. I am worthy of receiving everything I desire. Asking is feminine energy. My core value comes from my heart. I am anchored in my faith, family, and health. I am worthy of high-level energy. My worth comes from inside of my heart. I am grateful for this journey. I am the receiver of good energy.

What am I here to learn? I am here to receive everything I desire in life. I am love. Overthinking doesn't serve me. I can handle with grace anything that comes my way.

WEEK 49

– EMPOWERMENT

The Holy Spirit fills me with positive loving energy. I love myself. I give myself permission to give love and receive love freely. My strength is my feminine energy. I am experiencing emotions. My heart is my strength. I am here to surrender to my heart. I love myself. Staying grounded in my body is my strength. It's okay to feel this pain. It's good for me to experience every feeling, both good and bad. What am I here to learn? I am here to get inside of every moment. I'm the only one who can help myself. I am soft, sacred feminine energy. This is my truth.

– FEEL

I am committed to me. I trust in God's heavenly plan for peace and happiness. Today I finally understand a little more about making myself happy. I don't need others to make me feel happy or make me feel better. I've been using others to make me feel better about myself. I thought I was supposed to make others feel good. I understand that happiness comes from inside each of us. I need to think about me. I am happy. This journey is about me—and that I need to take a deeper look at myself. I have an abundance mindset. I need to do the things others aren't willing to do. I am willing to embrace where I am and find others to teach me what I don't know. I am smart. I have hope. Things are always working out for me. There is value in this journey. I don't have to figure it all out right this minute. It's getting easier and easier for me. This is where I'm supposed to be right now. I trust myself. I trust myself more than anyone. My only job is to live a happy life now. My heart is open. I trust me. I will look at myself. I am working on myself. I will be okay. I am connected to my feelings. I am connected to my heart. I am connected to the feelings in my body. I am healing. I deserve abundance. I honor myself. I deserve respect. I am radiant. The Holy Spirit fills my heart, and this is where my confidence is. All that ever was and ever will be is in my power now. I will be successful. I deserve success. I deserve abundance.

– TRUST

I show up for me. I trust in God's heavenly plan for happiness. I can handle everything. I trust myself. I trust everything is always working out for me. Trusting is my strength. How am I putting up walls? How can I fully surrender to my vulnerability? I will be okay. What if? What if my dreams don't manifest? I will be okay. My commitment to me is my top priority. I love myself. I am a loving person. I deserve abundance. I am grateful for this journey. I will be okay. I have a loving heart. I know that by trusting my heart, I give God the control, and I don't have to worry. "What if" is not an option.

– ACCEPTANCE

Trusting is my strength. I am grateful for this journey. I am grateful that I have found my confidence. I am grateful the Holy Spirit inspires positive energy inside of me. I surrender to God's plan for happiness. I am magnetic energy. Abundance flows to me easily and effortlessly every single day. Everything is okay. I meditate with love and joy. I am at peace with who I am and what I am becoming. I am a forgiven child of God. Everything I desire is being attracted to me. I am full of grace. I am soft, sacred feminine energy. I am the creator of everything I desire.

– RECEIVE

I am soft, sacred feminine energy. I am worthy of receiving everything I desire. I am a gift to others. I am the holder of valuable energy. I am the receiver of good energy. I am worthy of everything I desire. I am a good receiver. I am a high-value woman. I believe in my value. I am worthy of everything I desire. My purpose is staying connected to my heart. I have compassion for my heart. God has a plan. It hurts to feel helpless. I love myself. I have empathy for myself. I accept my feelings. I embrace my insecurities, my shame, my guilt. I am ready to be me.

WEEK 50

– EMPOWERMENT

Feeling into my confusion creates my strength. I am learning how to feel safe and secure. My brain needs to shut off and it's time to feel confidence from my heart and soul. My power and energy lie in my body. I am centered in my body. Trusting is my confidence. I am attracting everything I need into my life. I am pulling the whole world to me. My energy is my strength. My empowered life comes from connecting inside of me. I can experience the world from my true feminine center. This is my true power. I'm here to experience every moment and every pain. My pain is my strength. My pain makes my magnetic field stronger. My loving presence is my greatest gift. My inner feminine energy is my gift. I am who I am. I am unique and that's what makes me beautiful. I am worthy of abundance. I honor myself. I am always at my very best. I embrace where I am. I embrace. I am a powerful dynamic woman. I am a mountain on the inside. I am fully present to my own energy. I am fully present to my vulnerability and my feminine energy. I protect my open heart.

– FEEL

I am committed to me. I am so tired. I'm overwhelmed. I'm afraid. I am experiencing the problems of someone who is on her way to earning amazing abundance. I am at the same time finding myself. I am a high-value woman and I deserve respect. My heart is open. I honor myself. I trust in God's heavenly plan. The Holy Spirit shines in me. I love myself. Taking care of me and creating abundance is my priority. My heart is open. I can be me. I can let go of the negativity. If I feel fear, I take action. I can handle anything. I take care of me. I need to take care of myself. Trusting is my magnetic energy. My feelings are my power. How do I honor my feelings? I am grateful for this journey. I am learning patience and I am feeling my confidence getting stronger. I am filled with the Holy Spirit and I trust in God's heavenly plan for happiness.

– TRUST

Where do I not trust myself? I am committed to myself. Every time I feel fear is a reminder to feel my heart. Only I can make myself happy. My mind wants to create a solution, and I can't move forward until I feel comfortable. Being embarrassed doesn't serve me. I am good enough. I do trust myself. I deserve abundance. I deserve clarity. I am gentle. I am cherished. I am sensitive. I am vulnerable. My heart is open. My strength is my heart. I love myself. I protect my inner child. The Holy Spirit fills me up. I am grounded. I am smart. I am strong. I have an abundance mindset. I trust in God's heavenly plan for peace, joy, and happiness.

– ACCEPTANCE

I am attracting everything I want in my life. I am a receiver of good energy. Surrendering is my strength. I am grateful for this journey. I am attracting everything I need. Things are always working out for me. I trust in God's heavenly plan for happiness. The Holy Spirit fills me with deep joy, deep love, deep happiness and deep abundance. I am worthy of abundance. Abundance flows to me easily and effortlessly every single day. I am the source of everything I want. I show up for me. Abundance shows up for me.

My heart is full of love. I regenerate love and abundance inside of me. I am the creator of everything I desire. I am worthy of abundance. It's okay to allow love, joy, and abundance in my heart. I am worthy of everything that comes my way because of how I feel inside of me. I am soft, sacred feminine energy. I honor my goddess energy inside of me. I am warm and soft. I am loving. I am grateful. I am worthy of abundance. I love my life. I am grateful for my life and for this amazing journey. I trust in God's amazing plan.

– RECEIVE

I am worthy of receiving abundance. I am worthy of receiving positive energy. I am the holder of beautiful valuable energy. I am the receiver of good energy. I am worthy of everything I desire. I am a good receiver. I receive everything with deep joy. I am valuable energy. I am a high-value woman. I am a beautiful person. I am soft feminine energy. My value comes from inside of my heart. I am the receiver of good energy. My worthiness comes from staying connected to my heart. My purpose is staying connected to my heart. I am manifesting everything I desire.

WEEK 51

– EMPOWERMENT

I live in the present. I make time for me. I am becoming more of who I am by experiencing my feelings. I am connected to my true inner wisdom. I am grounded in myself. My true power is recognizing the experience of getting inside of every moment. My power is feeling all the sensations in my heart. Feeling pain and all my emotions makes me stronger. Everything is always working out for me. God has a plan—and I'm here to trust in it. I surrender to my purpose. My purpose is staying connected to my heart. What am I here to learn? I am here to play in the moment. I am enjoying the process. I know my value. All I need to do is be myself. I feel good about myself. I am amazing and magnetic. I light myself up from the inside. Only I can make myself feel safe and secure. *God's plan of abundance for me is way better than I can ever imagine.*

I can handle anything that comes my way. Worry does not serve me. Overthinking doesn't serve me. Staying stuck in my head doesn't serve me. Feeling my heart is where I find my confidence. My mind is an electrical field that tries to solve things. My mind doesn't want to listen to my heart. My inner wisdom and confidence come when I experience every moment. When I feel off, jumping to conclusions isn't where I find my confidence. My empowered life comes from inside of me. I step into my true power when I keep my body active and moving. Physical activity like walking or running helps me tap into my energy so I can move out of my mind. Experiencing my feelings and my energy is where I find my self-confidence.

– FEELING

What am I feeling? I want to run away from my feelings. Feeling my emotions is my strength. I am authentic. I am transparent. I attract only people who match my energy. Everything is going to be okay. My feelings are my power. My heart is my confidence. I show up for me. I attract only positive energy. I am building my relationship with myself. I trust my intuition. Ignoring my feelings doesn't serve me. I am grateful for my experiences that have made me a deeper, stronger energy. I honor my heart. I honor my feelings. By honoring my feminine energy, I honor myself.

– TRUST

Trust needs to be built inside of me. I need to trust myself first. Where have I put myself in compromising situations? Every experience, both positive and negative, have anchored me to finding myself. It all starts with me and trusting myself. My past does not define who I am in the future. What I'm learning now is showing me what I'm ready to learn. I can trust that all my struggles are here to make me a deeper soul so I can handle anything. When I trust myself, I can trust anything that comes my way. Outside situations will have nothing to do with my self-worth because I am anchored in my own energy. All challenges are here for me to learn. As I step into difficult situations, I will be okay because I am grounded in myself and my self-trust. Trusting in life allows me to learn and become deeper, knowing everything is always working out for me. I have the ability to turn pain into power. Every single thing that comes my way is an opportunity for me to step into my higher truth.

– ACCEPTANCE

Things are happening exactly the way they are supposed to. I trust this path of allowing. Allowing offers an opportunity for me to grow. I'm given everything I need. I trust and I know this is where I am supposed to be, and that I can't change anything or anyone. How will taking care of me bring me closer to finding abundance? I don't have to go out and get what I want. Things are always working out the way they are meant to be. I am inspired to take care of myself. I don't need to know the solution. The Holy Spirit fills me up. I make the time to be open to this.

– RECEIVE

How do I receive? What does this mean? First, I am worthy of receiving good energy. Shutting myself off because I don't understand doesn't serve me. How can I be a better receiver? What if I'm afraid to receive? What if I simply don't understand how to receive? What am I here to learn? When I am open to receiving, experiences elevate me. I am always receiving, which automatically makes me a good receiver. Nature gives to me. I am open to receiving just because of who I am. I don't understand this, but I don't need to understand.

WEEK 52

– EMPOWERMENT

What am I here to learn? The feelings I experience make me stronger. My awareness is anchored to my feelings. The world is attracting everything I desire towards me because I am choosing to experience my feelings. I acknowledge that my vulnerability and transparency is my greatest gift to others. The energy I feel on the inside is what others feel when they are with me. When I experience these feelings, I am creating my strength. My energy is what attracts others towards me.

Solutions don't come when I'm stuck in my head. Confidence comes when I feel good, and when I embrace the feelings of every moment. Staying present with myself anchors me in my truth. Staying present with myself creates a magnetic energy. My magnetic energy naturally attracts everything I need in my life. My purpose is staying connected to my heart. Staying grounded in myself empowers me to be more of me. My empowered life comes from how I feel inside of me.

– FEELING

What are the feelings I am feeling? Fear, anxiety, hurt, embarrassment, shame, regret, annoyance, happiness, love, joy, abundance, and positive energy are all strong emotions. Working through these emotions make me stronger. I am becoming stronger every day. I am becoming more of me. I am a leader. I am an influencer. Everything will be okay. I trust in God's heavenly plan for happiness. I am healing. I forgive myself. I am becoming stronger. I honor my heart. My loving presence is my gift to others. Making time for myself allows me to experience my emotions. Feeling every emotion creates strength.

– TRUST

What experience in my past have I ignored that has prevented me from stepping into my true power? If something doesn't align with my truth, it's important to remove myself from the situation. When others follow through on their commitments with us, it makes us trust them. That's where trust develops. When we show up for ourselves and keep commitments to ourselves, that's how we create trust in ourselves. Building trust begins on the inside. As I become more trusting in myself, I become more trusting in my relationships. My vulnerability and sensitivity are my power and my gift to the world. Feeling my vulnerability makes me stronger and builds trust in myself. I am building trust in myself first. By trusting myself and trusting in God's plan, I am becoming a deeper soul. Trusting that everything will be okay is trusting my intuition. Trusting my intuition builds my confidence. Every day I remind myself I am trustworthy.

– ACCEPTANCE

God has a timeline, and I accept it because I am worthy of happiness and fulfillment. I am committed to me. I am at peace with where I am. I am committed to understanding that I am not in control. I accept myself for who I am. I am bigger inside of me, something bigger than I could ever imagine. I am grateful for this journey, and know this has opened a door to many, more unimaginable things. I am no longer going to try to force my way in life. I surrender to God's plan. Everything I want is being attracted to me. All my power comes from the Holy Spirit. I surrender to my softness. God has a better plan than I could ever imagine. I am attracting everything I desire. Trusting God's timeline allows me to build confidence.

– RECEIVE

Because I don't know how to receive, doesn't mean I can't receive. Receiving starts with taking care of myself. All I can do is take care of me and nurture my heart. My power lies in my ability to receive. Knowing I am worthy, makes me a good receiver. I am a magnet attracting everything I desire. My worthiness comes from my heart. As the holder of beautiful, valuable energy, this makes me a good receiver. I am worthy of abundance. As I believe in my high-value energy, I am worthy of amazing things. Everything comes to me naturally with ease and grace. My truth allows me to attract everything I am worthy of so I can receive more abundance. My truth is that I value myself as a beautiful person. My value and worth does not come from what I can do for others. I am worthy of receiving everything I desire because of who I am. How do I receive? Knowing that I am worthy allows me to receive good energy and abundance. When I am open to receiving, the experience elevates me. I am a good receiver.

WHAT HAVE I LEARNED?

Congratulations! You have used my affirmations—and I hope that at some point you will create your own. Also, it is very beneficial for you to start journaling. Your super hero has been waiting for you. Remember, your confidence doesn't come from others, it comes from the inside. You deserve to celebrate!

I am soft, sacred feminine energy. My self-confidence comes from my feminine power. My feminine energy is magnetic. Everything I desire is being attracted to me. My empowered life does not come from the external world. My hero is deep inside of myself. Every day my hero needs to be reminded what to believe. My hero shows me how safe and secure I can feel. When we can love ourselves, we become a hero. A super hero. The time we give to our hero is priceless.

CONNECT ONLINE

LISARCARMICHAEL.COM

fb.com/lisarcar/

Instagram.com/lisarcarmichael/

www.LinkedIn.com/in/lisarcar/

ABOUT THE AUTHOR

How can I figure this out, I wondered. I was stuck and struggling knowing I deserved better and desperately wanting success. I knew it was up to me to make a difference, but I didn't know how—and honestly didn't know where to start.

I found myself overwhelmed, confused, and completely buried in debt. I was working a job which wasn't going to pay for two kids starting college. How would pouring myself into becoming an entrepreneur and a marketing professional support retirement in less than ten years? Months would pass, still no success and only more self-doubt.

I sat in my chair, trying to figure out this online business. Would things ever get better? Would I ever get a break?

Little did I know that I was on the verge of my big breakthrough—a breakthrough that anyone who has been struggling can easily create for themselves. My breakthrough came because I started a journal and affirmations.

When I was growing up, I never imagined becoming an author. I had no self-confidence. My only real goal was to graduate from high school. I graduated from college at the age of 30 with nothing more than a degree in marketing. I never had a dream to write a book or even where I would find success. In reality, I found myself stuck because that was what I was telling myself.

Lisa Carmichael is an entrepreneur and marketing professional who lives in Minnesota. She's a dedicated wife, a military spouse, and the mother of three adult children. Their transition into adulthood and the step into an empty nest was part of this journey of finding herself.

Lisa's passion is helping others also find themselves…and she works with people who are looking to find their own confidence and self-esteem.

Notes